Life of a Hostie: Everything you Need to Know to Become Cabin Crew

Hayley Stainton

First published November 2015.

Author Biography : Hayley Stainton (MSc (ESRC); PGCE; BA (Hons); TEFL)

Hayley is a tourism and aviation academic who, through her degree level lectures, website and personal mentoring, has helped hundreds of prospective Crew to secure their dream jobs with leading airlines across the world.

Having gained her experience as cabin crew whilst working for a leading UK airline, Hayley is now a Senior Lecturer in Tourism and Aviation specialising in a number of fields including *working as cabin crew*.

Preface

Is Cabin Crew your dream job? Do you want some 'insider tips'? Do you want to know what to expect? 'Life of a Hostie' is the ultimate guide, providing you with everything you need to know in order to confidently secure and commence a job as Cabin Crew.

For many, securing a job as Cabin Crew is the biggest challenge. From tips on how best to write your application form through to what to wear for your assessment day or how to prepare for your interview, you will feel much more prepared after reading the first chapter of the book.

The second hurdle is the Cabin Crew training-contrary to public opinion, Crew are far more than waitresses in the sky! From fire-fighting, to midwifery, to survival techniques, Cabin Crew are often the only emergency services at 30,000ft. Many Crew describe their 6+ weeks intensive training course as 'the toughest thing they've ever done' whilst also being 'by the far the most fun they've had'. It's hard work, but worth it- and chapter two will help you to be prepared and relieve some of those anxious nerves!

The final part of the book covers everything that you need to know once you start life as Cabin Crew. When working in the world of Aviation it can feel like everybody is speaking an entirely different language at times! This chapter covers all of the acronyms and phrases you will need to know, what to expect from shifts, working positions and duties, rosters and much more.

'Life of a Hostie' is designed to answer the many questions that job seekers, assessment day hopefuls and soon-to-be Crew have and to help you secure that life changing, dream job!

Contents

Introduction.. 10

Chapter One: The Application Process

Applying for a Job as Cabin Crew... 16

Research and Preparation..16

Skills and Qualities 18

Qualifications and Experience... 22

Age.. 24

Budget, Charter and Scheduled Airlines: What's the Difference?.......25

The Application Form.. 28

Telephone Interviews... 31

Assessment Days..32

The Result...43

Airport ID and Security Checks.. 44

Chapter Two: Training

The Training Course.. 48

Pre-start date Training and Preparation................................48

Essential Cabin Crew items and Shopping............................. 49

Accommodation, Hours and Costs....................................... 52

Your First Day.. 54

Customer Service Training.. 55

SEP Training..59

AVMED Training...73

Aircraft Types.. 77

Passing the Training Course................................. 79

Supernumerary Flight..80

Airline Terminology...81

Passenger Codes..85

Airport Codes...86

Airline Codes..88

Chapter Three: Life in the Skies

Working as Cabin Crew.......................................92

Money...92

Rosters...97

Pre-Flight Briefings.. 99

Cabin Crew Duties... 100

Working Positions..105

Classes... 107

Uniforms...107

Changing Jobs...111

Promotion Prospects..111

In Flight Assessments....................................... 111

Pregnancy and Babies.......................................112

Celebrities.. 113

Time Down Route...113

The Highs and Lows of being Cabin Crew..................... 115

Conclusion..117

Introduction

Many people aspire to work as cabin crew for the glamour, the travel and the potential to deliver a high-class service onboard an aircraft. However, for many, there are lots of unanswered questions regarding the position. Cabin crew is indeed a job like no other and life in the skies can feel like it is a world away from a 9-5 job down on the ground. Choosing to work as cabin crew is not 'just a job', it's a life style change.

For many, simply breaking into the aviation industry can be a challenging and daunting experience. Lots of preparation should be done prior to completing your application with regards to the aviation industry and its structure, the airline you are applying to work for and the job role itself. You may also need to develop your CV and gain relevant experience, such as working in a customer service based role prior to completing your application.

One of the most heavily discussed cabin crew topics appears to be surrounding assessment days. As the assessment day recruitment method is fairly unique to the role of cabin crew, many people feel like they are entering a black hole, as they do not know what to expect! However, although it can be a daunting experience, assessment days can also be really fun. This guide explains the entire process and provides tips on how to be successful.

One of the biggest hurdles to becoming cabin crew is passing the initial training and despite coming so far, many crew unfortunately do not make it through this final stage of the recruitment process. This guide aims to answer all of the questions that you may have regarding your initial training, from the topics that will be covered, the ways you will be assessed and the new terminology that you will be introduced to. It also provides you with insightful tips on things to revise/research prior to your start date, items that you may want to purchase and skills that you may want to improve.

Working as cabin crew offers many opportunities that no other job can provide, such as global travel, the chance to work for a world renowned airline and to provide a high standard of service and even the occasional opportunity to meet celebrities! No two days working as cabin crew are ever the same and you will work with a range of different people from different backgrounds and cultures. You will also be highly trained in the event of an emergency and if needed you will be the onboard doctor, psychologist, firefighter, policeman (or woman) or even midwife!

You are the 'face of the airline' and as such are expected to be well presented and deliver high class service at all times. Working as cabin crew can be hard work, but it can also be an incredibly enjoyable, fun and rewarding career... it is no wonder that demand to become cabin crew is so high! Whether you aspire to work for a budget airline such as easyJet or Ryan Air, a charter such as Thomas Cook, or a scheduled airline such as Virgin Atlantic, Emirates or British Airways, this guide provides all of the essential information to help you get through the application process, training course and to become a successful crew member!

Chapter One : The
Application Process

Applying for a Job as Cabin Crew

Your path to becoming cabin crew can be a long one, but it is without doubt a journey well worth entering once you have secured your dream job! From writing the application form, to making sure you have the correct qualifications and experience, to what to wear for your interview. This chapter will provide you with all of the essential knowledge you need when applying to become cabin crew!

Research and Preparation

The most important thing is to do your research. Not only should you know information about the airline you are applying for (such as what are the popular destinations they fly to or who owns the airline) you should also have an understanding of what the job is and what it entails, after all, you need to make sure that the job is 'for you'!

When working as cabin crew, airlines require their staff to be well prepared for everything. For example, you must pack everything you need for your trip, if you don't have a clean shirt for your return journey you could end up running to the dry cleaners or disguising the smell with excessive levels of perfume (which, by the way is not uniform standard- this will be discussed later on in Chapter Three). Onboard the flight you need to be well prepared as you are often on very tight, precise schedules. For example, if you do not remember to start heating the meals before takeoff, you might not have time to cook them and serve them on the flight! Furthermore, you need to be prepared for pre-flight briefings- you must have done your revision (again this will be discussed further in Chapter Three) and have remembered your passport and airport ID... or you won't be going anywhere!

Having good organisational skills are integral to any airline, and as such they will be assessing these skills from the moment you first contact the airline - your application. Therefore, it is important that you know your stuff. Why have you chosen to apply for that particular airline? What are the benefits of working for them? Find out about their history, the routes they fly to, the staff terms and conditions, the ethos of the company etc. It is a good idea to spend some time thoroughly researching these things not only for the benefit of your application, but also for yourself.

If you have never worked in the airline industry or studied one of the many aviation or cabin crew courses available, make sure you have good background knowledge before you start applying for jobs. Here are some things you might want to research;

    ✈ What are the differences between the 3 main types of airlines (budget, charter and scheduled)?

    ✈ What airlines dominate the industry?

    ✈ What mergers/alliances have recently taken place?

    ✈ What is the ethos of the airline you are applying to work for?

    ✈ What is the history of the airline you are applying to work for?

    ✈ What is your airline looking for in a cabin crew member?

    ✈ What are the main job roles for cabin crew?

    ✈ How many staff does your airline employ?

The first step to commencing a career as cabin crew is to understand the job role and the industry you aspire to work within. The internet is a valuable source of information for this, so it is recommended that you have a look around and see what you can find. There are a number of websites and forums such as www.lifeasabutterfly.com that include descriptions of personal experiences whilst working as cabin crew. www.cabincrew.com is particularly useful and if you browse through the different threads, they have a range of posts and discussions, from where is the best place to buy cabin shoes, to who is waiting for a start date with their airline. This is also a particularly useful place to make friends (virtually), before potentially meeting them in the skies!

Skills and Qualities

Airlines can be very particular when hiring their cabin crew as they will often have thousands of applicants for just a few places - so competition is high! They have very strict requirements with regards to the skills and qualities that they are looking for, and if you do not demonstrate these skills and qualities in both your application form and assessment day/interview, unfortunately you will not be securing your job in skies just yet.

Many people have the required skills and qualities; however they may not showcase these when they need to. Below is a summary of the key skills and qualities that airlines look for in their cabin crew.

✈ Customer service skills
This is an absolute essential. All airlines want their crew to provide a high level of service and you will need to demonstrate your customer service skills in your application. Have you ever encountered a difficult customer? Have you ever solved a problem? Do you have examples of times when you have delivered excellent customer service? If not, close this book and go and get some experience, because no airline will offer you a job.

✈ Teamwork skills
When working as cabin crew you will always be part of a team. Whether you are in a group of three people on a little A319, or one of twenty-four onboard an A380, teamwork skills are integral to the role of cabin crew.

During your day to day job you will be working closely with your crew. On each flight you will be given a role (usually a number related to hierarchy and experience), and this will determine your specific responsibilities. For example, a number seven may be responsible for completing security checks in the OHAR (overhead crew rest area), a number ten for handing out children entertainment packs and a number two in charge of the PAs (personal announcements). For a successful flight it is important that crew work together, take on the appropriate work loads, communicate effectively and demonstrate overall good team work.

Aside from a crew member's day to day tasks, they must also be prepared for any number of possible emergencies. For example, if your colleague finds somebody having a heart attack in their seat, do you think they would want help from another cabin crew member? Of course they would! When you are flying over the Atlantic at 30,000ft there may not be any doctors, or police, or firefighters onboard - so you and your team need to be prepared to switch from customer service mode to emergency mode at any given moment. Cabin crew have very strict training (this is discussed in Chapter Two) and have teamwork drills that they will undertake in an emergency. For example, if there was a fire, the person that finds the flames becomes the 'firefighter', they then call a second crew member who will become the 'communicator' and a third member will become the 'co-ordinator'. Each crew member has specific duties that they must undertake as part of the drill.

So, can you see why airlines look for teamwork skills in their prospective crew members? Being able to work as a team is vital, and your teamwork skills will often be assessed during a group activity on your assessment day. You will also need to go to your interview prepared with lots of examples of when you have demonstrated great teamwork.

✈ Communication skills
Being able to communicate with your crew and passengers is very important. Airlines will look for people that are approachable, clearly spoken, chatty and friendly. Many airlines will test your speaking skills through a PA assessment at your interview, whereby you will need to demonstrate that you can read the script given to you sufficiently.

✈ Initiative
Anything can wrong onboard an aircraft, from the wrong meals being loaded, to the in-flight entertainment not working, to a bomb threat. When working as cabin crew no two days are ever the same. It is for this reason that airlines are looking for people that have initiative. They want people to be able to think on their feet, and provide the best possible service to their customers in any given situation.
✈ Problem solving skills

Is a passenger's chair broken? Is there is a shortage of coke cans on the flight? Is there a drunk and disorderly passenger onboard? Has a pregnant lady gone into labour? It doesn't matter what the problem is, how big or small it may be, as cabin crew you need to do your best to solve it!

✈ Polite and friendly approach

Airlines will look for people that are polite, smiley and friendly. The top tip for assessment days is definitely to smile! Airline recruitment staff will be watching you from the moment you walk through the door and they want to see that you are the type of crew that would be polite and friendly to their passengers.

✈ Well groomed

Grooming is very important to all airlines, although perhaps some more so than others. British Airways even have reference to their grooming in their BA brand behaviours, stating that all crew must 'look the part'. This is not just about wearing the uniform, it's about having neat nails, hair and make up etc. Some airlines will even ask you to provide a photo as part of your initial application to prove that you are well groomed!

✈ Flexibility and adaptability

Want to go to yoga every Wednesday morning or out on the town every Saturday night? Forget it! The life of a cabin crew member changes every day, one week you might be in Los Angeles, the next in Nairobi.

Made plans for when you land back home? Think again! There are a number of reasons why you may finish work late. Your flight could go 'tech' down route causing you to stay away another night, your flight could be diverted because of a medical emergency causing you to land in a different destination or you could just simply be delayed.

As cabin crew you never know where you may end up, and one of the most common times this occurs is during standby shifts. This is when you literally 'stand by', whether it be at home or at the airport. And then at the drop of a hat you will be required to rush to an aircraft to get on a flight to… who knows where!

The airline industry is dynamic and ever changing, and you need to demonstrate as crew that you can work in such an environment.

✈ Attentive
Airlines want their crew to provide an efficient service - always. This will require you to be alert and on hand to the passenger's needs.

✈ Energetic
Working as cabin crew is a very demanding job. Did you know that one hour working work at 30,000ft has the same effect on your body as two hours working on the ground? As crew you could be working through the night, you could have very long days or you could have a particularly demanding set of passengers. During these times airlines want their crew to continue to look fresh, to smile and to be energetic.

✈ Punctual
If you are even a few seconds late for check in, a stand by crew member will be called and you will be reprimanded. There is no negotiation when it comes to punctuality as cabin crew. The flight must leave on time (aside from the obvious unavoidable delays), and as such you must be on time for work.

Late for your interview? You might as well turn back and go home, airlines do not want crew that are not punctual.

✈ Organised
As cabin crew you need to ensure that you have the required things with you for each flight. As a guide this is likely to include your passport; airport ID; aircraft manual; red notices; gillet or waistcoat; cabin shoes; spare tights; lipstick and anything else you may choose to carry with you. You will also need to be organised in-flight from preparing meals on time, to ensuring you place the correct items on your trolley. The airline you are applying for will want to see evidence that you are organised.

✈ Ability to work under pressure
From delivering a full meal service on a thirty minute flight from London-Paris, to dealing with a large number of drunk passengers demanding more alcohol on route to Las Vegas, cabin crew will often need to work to deadlines and under pressure. Airlines will look for this quality in their prospective crew and may ask for evidence of this during the interview process in the form of specific examples of your prior experience.

✈ Numerical competence
From working out the time in a new time zone, to calculating how long until landing, to working out currency exchange and counting change, all cabin crew need to have basic numeracy skills. Many airlines will ask for a C grade GCSE in maths or they may have a short numeracy test as part of the application process.

Terrible at maths? You might want to get practicing before your interview!

✈ Swimming competency
As part of CAA regulations all crew are required to demonstrate that they can swim at least 25 meters and that they are able to tread water for a short period of time. This is something that many aspiring crew worry about unnecessarily- as long as you can swim a short distance you will be fine, but if you're not very confident it might be worth organising some swimming lessons!

Qualifications and Experience

Each airline will have their own specific criteria, however as a rule of thumb, the following are standard requirements in order to stand a chance at becoming cabin crew;

✈ Maths and English
In general, most airlines will want their crew to have at least a level two qualification in English and maths (GCSE or equivalent), although some are stricter than others. Some airlines may choose to assess your

competencies themselves through testing as part of the application process, although many now will ask you to provide original exam certificates. Check with the individual airlines to see what their specific requirements are.

✈ Travel and tourism / cabin crew qualifications

Many colleges and further education providers now offer various courses that can help prepare you for a career as cabin crew. These can be very beneficial for enhancing your knowledge of the industry and the role of cabin crew, however undertaking such a course is not a necessity to secure a job.

✈ Degree

Have you ever heard cabin crew being referred to as trolley dollys? Do you think all they do is look pretty and serve tea and coffee, chicken and beef all day long? Think again!

Although having a degree is not a requirement for cabin crew, a surprisingly large amount of crew do have higher level qualifications in a wide range of subjects. This may also help you for future promotions or developments within the company and elsewhere, should you wish to move on from working as cabin crew eventually.

✈ Customer service experience

Examples, examples, examples – that is what airlines will ask for! Customer service is an integral part of the role of cabin crew and is very important to the airline. Whether you are applying to work for a budget airline, or a world class carrier, they will all want you to be able to demonstrate your customer service experience.

Your experience doesn't need to be within the airline or tourism industries either; it can be anything that involves working with customers. Many newly appointed cabin crew come from supermarkets such as Asda or Waitrose, waitressing jobs or working on reception desks at their local doctors surgery for example. If you have worked with customers, then you tick the box!

Airlines recruitment staff LOVE to hear all about your past experiences. They will want to know about how you can work as a team, deal with difficult customers, solve problems, demonstrate a high standard of service and lots more - so go to your assessment day or interview with lots of examples ready to give.

Age

Many people believe that the role of cabin crew is for young people. In fact, some countries such as Spain do not hire crew over a particular age. However, in Britain this is very much a myth, as airlines will generally hire the people that they believe are best for the job, regardless of age. British Airways for example has a mature crew base on some of their routes, and with maturity comes knowledge and experience - just because you may not be 21 any more does not mean you are not eligible to apply!

Many people decide to change careers later in life and cabin crew can be a very appealing option. Many crew members that may have had previous careers such as teaching, nursing or hairdressing for example, decide to swap their lives on the ground for one at 30,000ft.

On the other hand, many young people also chose to become cabin crew. Virgin Atlantic and British Airway's new Mixed Fleet for example, both consist of a large number of young crew, many of whom may be only 18 and just finished school. There are many benefits to airlines hiring young staff as they demonstrate a keen enthusiasm, are very motivated and energetic and are often still in 'learning mode' - ready for their training and exams. Furthermore, despite cabin crew salaries often being low in relation to other jobs (this will be discussed in Chapter Three), young people might not have the same financial commitments as they often choose to live at home with their parents and do not have any dependents.

Budget, Charter and Scheduled: What's the Difference?

When applying for a job as cabin crew it is important that you understand the industry you are aspiring to work in and the types of airlines that you may be applying for. Below is a brief outline of the three major types of airlines;

✈ Budget airlines

Many people look down on budget airlines due to their 'budget' approach and reputation, however they can be a very good choice of airline to work for, it all depends on what you want from the job!

A budget airline, also known as a low cost or no frills carrier is essentially an airline that offers few luxuries, in return for low prices (although these prices are not always as low as you might think!). These airlines have demonstrated huge growth over the last decade and have dominated many routes across Europe and worldwide. They have made competition very high and many scheduled airlines have struggled to compete. Many budget airlines will fly to/from 'cheaper' airports such as London Luton as opposed to London Heathrow, because the landing fees and taxations are lower. They also have a big push on in-flight sales, meaning that as crew your job role would have a heavier emphasis on selling items than it might for a scheduled or charter airline.

Budget airlines tend to operate predominantly short haul / European flights, therefore as cabin crew these are the flights you would be working on. They also have various means to cost saving such as short turnaround times and a lack of cleaning contracts, meaning that the crew will be required to clean and turn around the aircraft on landing quickly.

Budget airlines might offer competitive salaries, but they do often require their crew to work very hard. For instance, when working for easyJet you may work a six-hour flight to Sharm El Shiekh (Egypt) and back (and don't forget about the extra hours before departure and during turn around). Whereas if you were working for British Airways you would most likely work only one sector (i.e. London to Sharm El Shiekh).

Although working only one sector may be preferable, it means that you will have to night stop (stay the night away from home). So for example, if you worked a flight from London to Sharm El Shiekh as British Airways crew you would stay in Egypt for the night before returning back to London the next day. Whereas, whilst working for a budget airline such as easyJet you may have a longer day at work, but you will return home at the end of the day.

Many people choose to become cabin crew for the opportunities to see the world, and for those people airlines that give them the opportunity to have lots of night stops are often perfect. However, other people may get homesick, or have a family that they need to get home to at the end of the day, so airlines will minimal night stops may be more beneficial.

Budget airlines try their utmost to reduce their costs, this means that if you work for a budget airline you are likely to be based at an airport slightly outside of the city centre (e.g. London Luton), have more there and back flights (without a night stop) and have longer working days.

Each budget airline will work differently. easyJet for example, offers their crew permanent contracts, whereby although your roster will change each month, you will have guaranteed hours and a salary. Ryan Air however, often offer their crew 'zero hours' contracts. This is when they are under no obligation to give you a certain amount of flying hours within the month and your salary could be small, or potentially nonexistent if you are not given any hours at all.

Additionally, Ryan Air are known for charging their cabin crew for their training and uniforms and some airlines may charge in excess of £2000 for this. Whereas this is a staff benefit within most airlines, for Ryan Air it is another cost saving method. These costs will be taken out of the cabin crew's salary each month and if they choose to leave the company before they have paid back the amount owed they will be in debt to the company.

One of the benefits of working for a budget airline is often the salary. They may pay slightly more as a result of cost saving on aspects such as fewer hotels down route needed and no free crew meals onboard, that may be a staff benefit for other airlines. Budget airlines generally place a big emphasis on selling, and traditionally, with lots of selling comes lots of commission! You can find more details on earning money as cabin crew in Chapter Three.

✈ Charter airlines

A charter airline is one that does not run to a particular schedule. They have the flexibility to cancel and change flights depending on demand and can be chartered for ad-hoc flights by an individual company or operator.

Charter airlines are often associated with holiday packages, and popular airlines that cabin crew choose to work for include Thomas Cook, Tui and Monarch. Charter airlines differ from scheduled and budget airlines as they often offer seasonal contracts. After all, a huge number of Brits venture abroad in the summer months, therefore there will be more holiday flights operating. Many cabin crew fly during the summer months and choose to do alternative work during the winter, for example many may continue to work for their tour operator as a travel agent.

Charter airlines normally offer salaries in line with other airlines and will often recruit the same crew for several seasons. After you have gained experience you may also be hired on a permanent contract all year round, although securing permanent jobs are generally far more competitive.

Working for a charter airline can be beneficial; the majority of your passengers will be going on holiday and therefore are happy - and happy passengers often make for a happy crew! ☺ People are often also willing to spend when they are on holiday, so although charter airlines don't generally push sales as hard as budget airlines, you can make some reasonable amounts of commission.

Although whilst working for a charter airline you will often operate there and back routes, you may also get some night stops. One benefit is that charter airlines do not always offer frequent flights to all destinations so you may have to stay down route until the return flight is ready back - which may even be the same flight as the customers! Getting paid to spend a week in Cape Verde? Yes please!

✈ Scheduled airlines

A scheduled airline is one that works to a schedule, a bit like a bus- it always runs to the timetable regardless of how many passengers there may be. Scheduled airlines generally offer free food and drinks (most include alcohol, but not all) so there is less selling for the cabin crew to do. That also means less working out change and currency exchange!

Many crew aspire to work for the large scheduled carriers. They may start out working for a budget or charter airline to gain experience, but for many, their ambition is to fly for the likes of British Airways, Virgin Atlantic or Emirates!

Each airline offers different staff benefits and salaries, although they will generally include generous staff travel, free uniforms and training, free hotels down route and some even offer generous salaries.

The benefits of working for a scheduled airline include working for a large carrier with many routes and progression options and working for an airline with an international reputation. Getting a job with a scheduled airline can be very competitive; there are often thousands of applicants for just a handful of jobs!

The Application Form

The application form really is your first (and possibly last!) chance to shine! Airlines will strategically structure their forms to give you the opportunity to demonstrate all of the skills, qualities and experience that they are looking for in their cabin crew. Below are a number of tips for completing the form, and remember if you don't do a good job of the application form you won't make it to the next stage of the application process, so do your best!

Complete the form accurately

What you write on your application form will give the airline their first impressions of you. As competition is rife, application forms that are not completed accurately won't even get a second glance.

We all know that completing application forms can be a monotonous task, however you must ensure that you put in all of your effort here in order to secure yourself an interview or assessment day. It can be tempting to simply 'copy and paste' sections of application forms or your CV, but this often doesn't work and is often very obvious to the recruitment staff that will read it. This also often results in inaccuracies and parts being included that are not necessarily relevant to that particular application. So, the first tip for application writing is to start each application from scratch.

When you complete the form you need to make sure that all of the information you include is accurate. For instance, if you finished school in 2006, then make sure you find the specific date. Make sure you don't have any gaps in your employment history, and that your contact details for your references are correct. If there are any discrepancies your application may be discarded.

Employment history and reference details are particularly important when applying for a job as cabin crew as these will be required in order to get your airside pass (discussed further towards the end of Chapter One). So make sure they are completed accurately!

Write concisely

Nobody wants to read an application form the length of a book. Say what you have to say without 'waffling' and write concisely.

Spelling, English and grammar

Do you want the airline's first impression of you to be that you can't spell or that you have bad English? We all make mistakes, and it is often hard to spot them yourself, so get somebody to proof read your application before you send it off.

✈ Refer to the job specification

There will almost always be a job specification or description. For example, British Airways state on their website;

'Here at British Airways we provide fantastic opportunities for you to learn, develop and build upon a career. We as a fleet recognise hard work and high performance with rewards supporting possible promotions. You will be expected to work 365 days a year at various times of the day and night and crossing many time zones. Can you set a positive tone waking up at 3am after a short rest, be there for our customers and deliver an exceptional service with a smile? If you are a passionate individual who strives to keep the customer at the heart of everything you do and would like to contribute to our success, why not grab this exciting opportunity and apply today!'

The job description, or any information the airline may give about the role should be studied carefully prior to completing your application form.

This is a mistake that many people make when completing application forms. It's really quite simple, use it as a 'tick list' to ensure that you demonstrate that you have all of the skills, qualities and experience that they are looking for.

Firstly, take the job description and highlight the key words. Please find the example below.

'Here at British Airways we provide fantastic opportunities for you to learn, develop and build upon a career. We as a fleet recognize hard work and high performance with rewards supporting possible promotions. You will be expected to work 365 days a year at various times of the day and night and crossing many time zones. Can you set a positive tone waking up at 3am after a short rest, be there for our customers and deliver an exceptional service with a smile? If you are a passionate individual who strives to keep the customer at the heart of everything you do and would like to contribute to our success, why not grab this exciting opportunity and apply today!'

Once you have identified the key words, incorporate these into your application form. See the answer to the question below as an example.

Question- *Why do you want to work as cabin crew for British Airways?*

Answer- *I am a hard working, passionate individual who aspires to contribute to the success of British Airways. I always strive to provide an exceptional level of service and deliver a high performance within my work and I can see that the customer is always at the heart of British Airway's cabin crew. I want to work for British Airways as it is a company with an exceptional reputation that would offer me many opportunities for learning, development and promotion in the future.*

✈ Ask a friend to proof read

It is often difficult to spot your own mistakes, so once you have completed your application form, give the job specification/advert and your completed application to a friend or family member and ask them to check it over for you. They might notice things that you may have left out or spelling mistakes that you hadn't!

Telephone Interviews

Some airlines will require you to undertake a telephone interview prior to offering you an assessment day. An example is Qantas, who require you to pass a telephone interview on receipt of a successful application form. Telephone interviews are normally nothing to worry about and will be relatively informal. However, you will need to make sure that you are prepared with lots of those 'customer service examples' that were previously discussed.

Questions that you may be asked could include;

✈ Why do you want to work for this airline?

✈ Why would you be a good person to work as cabin crew?

✈ Tell me about a time when you demonstrated a high level of customer service

✈ Can you give me an example of a time that you have dealt with a difficult customer?

✈ How would you define good customer service?

Once you have passed the telephone interview you may be invited to an assessment day or formal interview.

Assessment Days

The big AD! Most airlines select their cabin crew through an assessment day process. This is a day that will consist of a number of activities, tasks and interviews. Below is a general structure of an AD, although of course this does differ between airlines.

✈ Arrival

You might not consider this as 'part of the day', but in actual fact it is probably the most important part! You are being watched from the moment you arrive. The airline wants to see that you are on time-lateness is not acceptable for most airlines, so if you are late you may as well turn around and go back home. Many people choose to stay the night before in a local hotel or will do 'dummy runs' to the airport to ensure that they know the route. Whatever you do, do not be late!

They also want to see the way that you interact and the first impressions you give. If you have ever attended an assessment day you will probably have noticed that you will have to wait around for a few minutes until the day 'officially' begins, but what you probably did not realise at this point is that it has already begun, and you are in fact being monitored and assessed already!

The recruitment team will be watching you. Do you stand in the corner alone or do you interact with the other candidates? Do you come across as smiley and friendly or are you unapproachable? Even if it doesn't come naturally to you to make conversation with people you do not know, make an effort for your assessment day as that is what airlines want to see!

🏃 Introduction to the airline
As part of your AD you will normally have some form of talk from the airline. They will provide a background of the company you are hoping to work for, they will explain the job role, duties, typical rosters etc. They will also give you the opportunity to ask questions.

Remember that you are being watched at every moment, so although you may simply be listening at this stage, make sure you are well presented, sitting up straight etc. For instance, do you think Virgin Atlantic would want to hire somebody that looked as if they were falling asleep during their presentation? Make sure you are alert!

Asking questions is very acceptable, but be careful. A simple bit of research prior to you interview will probably answer most questions that you may have, so don't make yourself look unprepared by asking questions that you should probably already know the answers to!

🏃 Height and weight testing
Most airlines have restrictions with regards to the heights and weights of their cabin crew. These are very important as they are directly related to the health and safety of the crew and passengers onboard. If you are too short to open the overhead lockers then how can you do your job properly? And if you are too tall and bump your head on the ceiling are you going to be able to work effectively? It is common sense really. Working in a confined space is a challenge for many people, and the airlines need to ensure that they hire only people who are physically able to do the job.

However, many people still insist on attending their assessment day, even though they do not meet the essential criteria. If this is you, do not bother- you will only be sent home!

Early on during the assessment day the airline will check that you meet the requirements. Some airlines ask for a specific maximum weight, and therefore may weigh you. Others ask for you to be able to comfortable secure yourself into a jump seat using the straps and will ask you to demonstrate that you are able to do this. Most airlines will have maximum and minimum height restrictions and will measure your height. Unfortunately if you do not meet any of the requirements you will then be sent home.

The requirements for each airline differ depending on the aircraft that the crew operate and the individual airline's specific preferences. For instance, a short haul carrier may have small aircraft and only require their cabin crew to be a minimum of 5ft tall, whereas an airline that owns some of the larger aircraft such as A380s or Boeing 747s will require their crew to be taller.

✈ Testing

Airlines may choose to test your competencies in particular things and will require you to undertake a test to demonstrate this. This could include for example a basic maths test to ensure that you would have sufficient ability to calculate change and exchange currencies.

They may also require you to undertake basic language tests or safety and security tests. Although you may not yet have all of the knowledge required to become cabin crew, the airline may want to test your ability to solve problems or for you to demonstrate your level of 'common sense'. They will often use testing to do this.

✈ Group tasks

Working as a team is an integral part of working as cabin crew and each airline will want to assess your team working abilities. There will usually be some sort of task that gives you the opportunity to work as a team. Use this as your chance to shine- they will be watching you!

Some examples of team work activities that have been used in cabin crew assessment days include;

   ✈ Create a radio advert for a holiday company with your team mates ready to present in 15 minutes.

🛫 Using the materials list provided, design a cabin crew uniform for your chosen airline, justifying your choices.

🛫 Using the lego bricks in front you create an object that is circular in shape, has wheels and can be used within the aviation industry.

Group tasks will not necessarily be challenges that can be completed, and there is not normally a 'right or wrong' result. They are simply giving you the opportunity to demonstrate that you can work in a team.

Below are some tips for the group tasks;

   🛫 Listen to others

   🛫 Do not be over-powering or controlling

   🛫 Speak, but also allow others to speak

   🛫 Encourage quiet members to join in

   🛫 Do not be bossy

   🛫 Listen to everybody's point of view

   🛫 Allow everybody a turn

   🛫 Do not talk over others

   🛫 Customer service activity

Customer service is another area that is very important for airlines, and they will require their prospective cabin crew to demonstrate their ability to provide a high level of customer service. Airlines will normally choose a roleplay situation for you to undertake as part of your assessment day.

An example of a typical roleplay could be you acting as a waitress serving a customer in a restaurant. The customer would normally have some kind of problem for you to solve and may be a difficult customer. You need to demonstrate that you can resolve the problem and provide good customer service. A problem could be something such as there not being any vegetarian options on the menu. A sufficient response would be for you to say that you could substitute meat from a particular meal with a vegetarian alternative, all the while being very helpful, smiley and professional.

Here are some things that airlines will be looking for within your customer service assessment;

🛫 That you are approachable

🛫 That you have initiative to deal with different situations

🛫 That you are polite

🛫 You are friendly

🛫 You are professional

🛫 You smile

🛫 You make the customer feel wanted

Airlines will not hire people that;

🛫 Are rude to the customers

🛫 Do not appear to be confident in what they are doing

🛫 Cannot solve problems

🛫 Are not approachable

✈ Are grumpy

✈ Make the customer feel unwanted or hard work

Your customer service assessment is your chance to shine, so make sure you do a good job! It may even be worth practicing these types of roleplays with somebody at home before your assessment day.

✈ PA assessment
An important part of working as cabin crew is reading PAs (personal announcements). Some airlines will require you to read aloud a PA to ensure that you have a professional pitch and tone.

In preparation for this, try reading aloud at home before your assessment day. You can also find some example PAs online to practice.

✈ Moment of truth
Many airlines will choose only a select few to proceed to the second part of the AD, which will normally consist of a formal interview. Based on the activities that you have undertaken in the first part of the day, you may be sent home. Airlines will often choose an 'X Factor' style approach, taking all those that have been successful into one room, and all those that have not into another. They will then break the news, meaning that some people will go home and some will stay for the interview.

Not all airlines choose to operate this way, for example British Airways insists on interviewing all of their applicants that make it through to an assessment day, however it is a popular practice.

✈ The Interview
The final part of the day will normally be the interview. This may be a panel interview, it may be 2 people interviewing you or it could be 1:1. The interview could last anything from half an hour to a couple of hours, depending on the questions that the airline chooses to ask and the responses that you give.

You will be assessed on your answers given, but also on the way you respond, your body language, and any questions that you may have. During your interview you may be very nervous, this is normal and the recruitment team will expect this, so don't worry, however some basic interview preparation may help.

Try practicing answering possible questions that may come up in advance. Questions could include things such as;

✈ What skills and qualities could you bring to the airline?

✈ Why do you want to work for this airline?

✈ Why do you want to be cabin crew?

Re-read the job specification and your initial application before your assessment day- what skills and qualities were they looking for again? Try to incorporate these into your answers, just as you did in your initial application.

You will also need to go to your assessment day with lots of examples. Airlines love to hear about your previous experiences and will want you to provide specifics, so prior to your AD have a good hard think! You may be asked things such as;

✈ Can you give an example of a time when you have demonstrated excellent customer service?

✈ Can you tell us about a time when you have had to solve a problem?

✈ Can you give an example of a time when you have demonstrated good teamwork?

Airlines will also often ask questions that are slightly more difficult and that have the potential to 'trip you up'. Examples could include;

✈ When have you felt disappointed with your performance at work?

✈ Can you give an example of a time when you have had to accept feedback that you have not been happy with?

✈ Working as cabin crew is a very demanding job in terms of working unsociable hours, being away from home for long periods of time and having disrupted sleep patterns. How would you cope with this lifestyle?

Believe it or not, these sorts of questions are not designed to trip you up, but they do require a little more thinking in order to ensure that you give an answer that puts you in a positive light.

For instance, in answer to the first question you could give an example of when you didn't do a very good job at work and were given negative feedback from your manager, however this wouldn't make you look very good. Alternatively, you could describe a time that due to external circumstances (i.e. a fire alarm went off and you needed to evacuate the building fast) you were not able to provide the level of service that you wanted to. The second answer makes you look far more positive than the first. It might be worthwhile having a think about some of these types of questions that could come up prior to your interview to help prepare you.

Whilst answering your questions maintain your positive attitude and good customer service skills. Smile LOTS, be friendly and approachable and try to relax. Make sure that you maintain good body language, don't have closed body language i.e. folding you arms and try to sit up straight. Remember- they are watching you ALL of the time!

✈ Appearance

Grooming and appearance are VERY important to airlines and it is imperative that you demonstrate that you would be able to wear the airline's uniform with pride. Throughout the day they will be assessing your appearance, so do not let it drop. Here are some tips;

✈ Hair

This must be neat. No unnatural colours and no roots if you dye your hair. Most females choose to put their hair up in a similar style to what the airline's crew would normally wear, for example a bun. If you do decide to put your hair up make sure it is very neat. For men, your hair must be neat and you must be cleanly shaven.

✈ Makeup

You should wear some form of makeup, although do not go over the top- remember you are at a job interview, not on a night out! Airlines will require their crew to look professional, so wear natural colours. Most girls will choose to wear a natural colour foundation (absolutely no orange faces!), blusher and subtle eye makeup. Large false eyelashes or bright coloured eye shadows are a definite no go. Many airlines require their crew to wear lipstick, so most people will choose to do so for their assessment day. Pinks or reds are generally acceptable. Don't let your make up standards drop throughout the day, reapply your lipstick and anything else that may require attention throughout the day!

Some men choose to wear a little natural looking makeup such as clear mascara, concealer or foundation.

✈ Perfume

We all like to smell nice, but don't overdo it! Too much perfume is not recommended, and would not be acceptable when working as cabin crew.

✈ Nails

Many girls will choose to have their nails professionally done or to paint them. Make sure you use appropriate colours, such as pinks or reds. Nails should be an appropriate length and not too sharp- you do have to work with them after all. Many men will also choose to use clear nail polish.

✈ Clothes

Most people will choose to wear clothes of a similar style to the crew of the airline that they are applying for. This means suits for men and a skirt and shirt combination or dress for a woman. Most people will wear a suit jacket. Many people choose to wear similar colours to their chosen airline's uniform too, for instance, you may choose to wear a red shirt with a black suit for an assessment day at Virgin Atlantic. This is popular, but not essential.

Whatever you choose to wear, make sure that it fits you well and is clean and ironed. Uniform standards are very important to airlines, and as such you need to demonstrate that you would be able to wear the uniform appropriately.

Men should wear ties and shirts should be tucked in. Women should wear tights if wearing a skirt/dress (you can wear trousers, although most girls choose not to). It is suggested that you take a spare pair of tights in your bag, you will be grateful if you acquire a ladder on route to the assessment centre!

✈ Shoes

Heels! Your airline will most likely require you to wear heels, so show them that you can wear heels! No higher than a few inches and a professional pair of shoes of course though, as said previously, you are not on a night out on the town!

If you are not used to wearing heels it might be an idea to practice walking around in them for a while before your AD!

✈ Piercings, jewelry and tattoos

Airlines will generally permit a small pair of earings or a small ring on each hand. If you have multiple piercings then you should take them out for your assessment day.

Airlines do not normally hire people that have tattoos in visible places. If you are planning on embarking on a career as cabin crew DO NOT GET TATTOOS. If it is already too late then you may have difficulty securing a job. It has been known for people to keep their tattoos hidden from their airlines after purchasing tattoo cover up products, however this is risky as if they catch you, you could end up facing dismal for not adhering to uniform guidelines. It has also been known for airlines to offer jobs on the condition that the tattoos are removed, this can be a timely process but is possible.

Assessment day top tips!

Baring in mind everything discussed, here is a list of top tips for your assessment day;

Be on time

Interact with others as soon as you arrive

Be friendly and smile

In fact, smile, smile, smile all day long!

Ask sensible questions

Look assertive, pay attention and keep up appearances throughout the day

Do some research before the day

Make sure your appearance is top notch all day

Demonstrate your skills as much as possible when given the opportunity

Have fun!

It may sound like a daunting experience, but believe it or not attending a cabin crew assessment day can be really good fun, even if you don't get offered a job at the end of it! Most people relax once they arrive and enjoy meeting new people and learning about the airline. It is an excellent experience and if you are not successful do not worry- count it as a practice run and try again next time!

The Result

Waiting to find out if you have been successful or not in your assessment day can be an nerve-racking experience. They may let you know the next day or they could leave you waiting for weeks. The important thing to remember is not to worry too much, if you are not successful this time you can always apply again.

Some airlines will phone you to offer you a position, some may write and others will send you an e-mail. You will generally be made aware of the process at your assessment day.

You can read about other people's assessment day experiences at www.lifeasabutterfly.com

Airport ID and Security Checks

Once you have secured a job as cabin crew you will undergo vigorous security checks. The airline will require five years worth of references and every day must be accounted for- any gaps and they will want to know why! You can use academic references, for example whilst you were at school, or employment references. These are not to check your character, but simply to check where you have been for the past five years.

The airline will also require a satisfactory CRB (criminal record bureau) check. You may be required to obtain this yourself, or the airline may do it on your behalf. If you do have nay previous criminal records you can still apply, but it is unlikely that you will pass the security checks.

Many cabin crew may not start their employment with their airline on the intended date as a result of their security clearances taking a long time, and in some cases they may never successfully obtain the references required for an airside ID and therefore will never start working as cabin crew. When completing the relevant paperwork for your ID make sure that you complete everything accurately to avoid any unnecessary delays!

Chapter Two: Training

The Training Course

So you have been offered a job as cabin crew- congratulations! But you are not there just yet! You will have been given a conditional offer, meaning that unless you pass the training course, you won't be working at 30,000ft any time soon. This chapter outlines all of the training that crew will have to undertake and some of the things that you may want to work on before commencing your official training to help give you a head start!

Pre-Start Date Training and Preparation

Believe it or not, the training actually begins BEFORE you start working for the airline! Most airlines will ask you to complete pre-start date work. This could include anything from aviation medicine to customer service training. This will often consist of a series of question and answer type tasks. For instance, British Airways provide their trainees with several documents outlining things such as their brand behaviours and customer service techniques. The trainee then needs to complete a number of questions, demonstrating their understanding.

Completing pre-start date work can be very useful. It helps you to begin to gain an understanding for the ethos, standards and procedures for the airlines will (hopefully!) be working for. It also helps to prepare you for the training ahead. If your airline doesn't require you to do any specific work prior to your start date, it might be worth undertaking your own research anyway. This will help to improve your knowledge and confidence for when you do start.

Many cabin crew will have to wait weeks, if not months between the time they are offered the job until the time they actually start. When you are excited, this can seem like forever, so why not use your time to make sure you are fully prepared for embarking on your new career?

This is the perfect time to begin to network, meet some people that you may be training with and learn a bit more about the job. Twitter is great for this and you can search hashtags such as #lifeofahostie or #crewlife to find relevant people to follow.

www.cabincrew.com is a great place to begin to network. They have airline specific forums, whereby you can join in discussions, read relevant information and get to 'virtually' meet some of your fellow crew. Many people will use this as a platform to meet people that will be on their training courses which can be very useful if you need to find somebody to share accommodation with during the training course.

Essential Cabin Crew Items and Shopping

While waiting for your start date, why not get prepared by buying some of the items that you may require as cabin crew. Below is a summary of some of the things that you may wish to invest in;

✈ Shoes

Some airlines provide shoes, others do not. If you are working for an airline that requires you to purchase your own shoes, it may not be as simple as you might think! For example British Airways asks their crew to purchase two pairs of shoes, both black with no patterns or stitching- NOTHING. One pair must have high heels (although not too high), the other must have a very small heel but must not be entirely flat.

Have you ever tried looking for shoes with such specific requirements? It's a challenge, that's for sure!

You will be spending many hours and walking many miles in these shoes, so it is important that they are comfortable- give yourself plenty of time to shop around.

✈ Visas

Depending on the routes you will be operating, your airline may require you to obtain certain visas. They will normally notify you of the requirements prior to your start date. These can be timely to obtain and may cost you money (although the airline will often pay/reimburse you). You may wish to spend time arranging these prior to your start date.

✈ Vaccinations

Again, depending on the routes that you will be operating, you may be required to have certain vaccinations prior to starting flying. This may include jabs such as;

- ✈ Hepatitis A & B
- ✈ Polio & Diptheria
- ✈ Yellow fever
- ✈ Japanese Encephalitis
- ✈ Rabies
- ✈ Tetanus

Yellow fever is a particularly important vaccination and some countries will ask you to provide evidence of your vaccination in the form of a certificate at immigration.

✈ Passport

Is your passport in date? If not, you better get renewing it!

✈ Business attire

During your training you will probably be asked to wear smart casual clothes for the first few weeks until you get your uniform. If you do not already have some suitable outfits it might be time to go shopping!

✈ Pen and paper

Remember, even after you have been offered the job as cabin crew, this is still dependent on you passing the training course. Make sure you are organised and come with some paper and pens. This might sound obvious, but it is something that many people don't think about when they imagine the beginning of their career in the skies!

✈ Cabin bag and suitcase

Most cabin crew will have two cases- a cabin bag and a larger suitcase. All cabin crew will be required to have a cabin bag, this must fit within the size restrictions given by the airline and will usually need to be black or another colour as directed by the airline.

Some airlines may provide you with suitcases, but for those that do not, you might want to think about getting organised before starting your training. Firstly, check the restrictions of your airline for size. Secondly, check if they have any other specific requirements, i.e. colour, material. It is recommended that you choose a hard wearing case; you will be need to get good wear out of your cabin bag, so this is not a time to count the pennies- buy quality! There is nothing worse than having a bag that doesn't stand up, or where the zip keeps breaking. Many people opt for a hard shell case as these are often more hardy.

You may or may not choose to use a second suitcase. Depending on where you may be travelling to and the period of time that you are away from base you might want more space or need to carry more things, For example, a cabin bag may be sufficient for a four day trip to New York in the summer, but in the winter you may require more space for large coats, boots etc. This is something to start looking into while you wait for your start date.

✈ Camera

It is quite likely that you will visit some magnificent places on your travels, so of course you will want to photograph them! It is recommended that you purchase a decent camera to capture some of those special moments!

✈ Laptop/i pad

Some destinations are less exciting than others and you may prefer to simply stay in your room and relax. Other times, you may be lying awake in the middle of the night due to the time difference. It is times like this that you will be grateful for your technology.

Most crew will take either a laptop, an i pad or equivalent with them on their trips. You can use these to watch films, to surf the internet, to play games etc. many airlines have special rates with some of the big technology providers such as Apple, so although this is something you may want to look into prior to your start date, you might want to wait until you are confirmed in post in order to get your discount!

✈ Kindle
You are likely to have lots of time on your hands as cabin crew. Time chilling around the pool in Ghana, sitting in your warm bed watching the snow outside in Denver, or even during crew rest on board the aircraft. It is at these moments that having a good book to read will come in very handy!

✈ Miniatures
As we all know, we can't travel with liquids in our carry on luggage. Therefore, it might be worth investing in some miniature pots that can be refilled with your favourite toiletries. Primark or Tesco are good places to buy these for just a couple of Pounds.

Accommodation, Hours and Costs

Many newbie cabin crew members are anxious about the first weeks of the job. Some of the key areas of concern are typically where they might stay, when they will be at work and how much money they might have (or have not) to spend.

✈ Training accommodation
Some airlines will provide you with accommodation during your training, others will not. As many crew will choose to commute to work (as they won't be driving on a daily basis due to stop overs, roster patterns etc) they may need a place to stay during the training.

There are various 'crew houses', where you can rent a room for a night, a weekend, a week or whatever you want really. Many crew choose to stay in these during their training. You can also rent a room in a crew house when you are flying, for example before early starts or when you have only minimum rest between flights.

Many people also choose to stay in a hotel. The Travel Lodge at Heathrow is a popular choice for crew training nearby as the prices are reasonable and it is close to many airline training centres. Crew will normally pair up and share a room to reduce costs. www.cabincrew.com is a great place to find other people from your training course and to choose to share a room with in advance.

Many hotels will give discounts to airline employees, so it is worth investigating pricing options before you commit too.

✈ Hours

While you are training you will work a lot of hours- be prepared to give up your social life for the duration of your course!

Your airline will dictate your start and finish times, although you never really finish until you graduate at the end. Each night you will be given 'homework' tasks or revision to do. You will normally train 5 days a week but this may be more, depending on the airline's requirements.

Upon completion of the training course you may not have any rest days before working your first flight- be warned!

The training course is very tiring and can be stressful, but it can also be great fun.

✈ Costs

Depending on your airline, you may be required to outlay some initial costs. This could include things such as purchasing a new passport, paying for visas or buying the essential cabin crew items listed above.
You will often not be paid full salary during your training and as such you may need to budget for this before hand. For example, at Virgin Atlantic crew are given an allowance when they travel and they will often use this boost their salary. They will not have this extra money given to them during their training. At British Airways crew are paid FDP (flight duty pay) during their time away from base (i.e. when they are flying and during stop overs), similarly, the crew will not have this money during training.

Other airlines, such as Ryan Air, may charge their cabin crew for the training they undertake. Although this will not normally be an initial cost, it is important that crew know that this may be deducted from their forthcoming salary.

Starting your career as cabin crew can be a stressful time, so don't let something like money contribute to any stress levels, put some money aside in the months before your start date to help you out when you may be paid less.

Your First Day

Congratulations the day has finally arrived!

Your first day in your dream job is a big deal, so make sure you are prepared! Below are some guidelines to help make sure that you begin your cabin crew career with a kick start!

✈ Plan your journey
Make sure you know where you are going. Perhaps do a dummy run to see how long it takes you and to investigate places to park. If you are travelling by public transport check out the train/ bus times in order to make sure that you will arrive on time. If you are based in the UK take an umbrella- you want to look good for your first day and you never know when the skies will choose to open!

✈ Pack all of your stuff the night before
The night before make sure that you are completely prepared. Pack your pens, paper and any paperwork you were asked to complete. Also bring any pre-start date work you have undertaken. Pack a spare pair of tights (if you are wearing tights) and your lipstick- start as you mean to go on with appearances!

✈ Leave yourself plenty of time
The last thing you want to do is arrive for your first day stressed. Make sure you arrive early. This will help relax you (you are probably already

nervous!), and will give you time to meet your fellow crew before beginning the training course.

✈ Make friends

You will be spending the next six weeks (or how ever many weeks your airline takes to train you) with these people- introduce yourself, make a good first impression and make friends!

✈ Dress professionally

You obviously won't have your uniform yet so make sure you dress in an appropriate way. You will probably choose to wear something similar to what you wore for your assessment day. Girls will often wear a skirt and shirt or blouse and men will normally dress in a suit. Girls may wear a dress or trousers if they prefer.

If you wear tights make sure you pack a spare pair- you never know when you might get a ladder and ladders do not look professional! Also pack some of your makeup. You should apply natural looking make up, similar to the way you looked at your assessment day, be sure to pack essentials like lipstick so that you can reapply throughout the day. Make sure your nails are clean and polished.

Your first day will normally consist of general introductions and an outline of the course that you are about to undertake. You will have a lot to take in and it is important to concentrate and focus throughout the day, but it is also important to enjoy it!

Customer Service Training

As part of your six week training course you will undergo customer service training. You have already demonstrated that you have good customer service skills, otherwise you wouldn't be where you are now! However, the airline will now need to train you to deliver the service in the way that they require.

This is where you will learn all about the airline, how they work, their procedures and their standards. This can be a challenging part of the training, as airlines can be very particular, but it can also be really good fun! You will learn a number of things during your customer service training, these are outlined below;

✈ Uniform standards

Uniform and grooming are very important to airlines as the cabin crew are the 'face of the airline'. Your airline will spend time during your customer service training explaining the uniform procedures and checking that you are dressed to correct standard. It is often during this time that you will get to wear your uniform for the first time, which can be very exciting!

Most airlines will be flexible on the first day that new entrants wear their uniform, however after day one is over they will be far more strict. It is common that new cabin crew are reprimanded for having the wrong denier tights, chipped nail polish or an untidy bun in their hair for instance. Uniform standards are very important and in extreme cases people that do not adhere do not successfully pass their training course. You can read more about uniform standards in Chapter Three.

✈ Brand behavior and the company's visions and goals

You will learn all about what is important to your airline, what they aim to achieve and the role that you will play in that as cabin crew. For instance, British Airways has a number of brand behaviours, all of which you must demonstrate whilst working as crew including 'looking the part', 'solving problems' and 'treating everyone as an individual'.

The brand and visions should be represented by the cabin crew at all times, and as such it is important that trainee cabin crew have a thorough understanding of the airline's ethos and values. You may be tested on this.

✈ Service standards

Airlines are very specific on the service that they offer and different airlines can vary significantly. Some airlines may have a casual approach, whereas others might offer a more premier service.

You will learn a huge amount during your customer service training and some airlines will put a heavier emphasis on this than others. For instance, if working for a budget airline such as easyJet, you may spend more time focusing on the selling skills as selling is a big part of what their crew do onboard the flight. Alternatively, if working for an airline such as Emirates, you will spend a substantial amount of time on the premier services offered onboard.

You will learn the service down to every last detail. Who should be served first, the lady in the aisle or the person closest to the window? How should you open the bottle of wine? Should you crack open the Coke can before giving it to the customer? Where should you stand during boarding?

Each airline is slightly different and you will learn all of the 'ins and outs' during your customer service training. It is important that you demonstrate your ability to deliver customer service to the required standard during your training and you will probably have a series of practical, role-play style assessments on this.

Service recovery

This is a very important part of customer service that you will have training on. It is important to remember that as hard as we might try to please them, there are times when customers may be unhappy with the service they have received, whether this is our fault or otherwise.

As the face of the airline, cabin crew are often the people that have to deal with passenger problems and complaints, even though they may actually have had nothing to do with the problem. Delays and problems at the airport are common examples. If you are delayed for six hours prior to boarding your aircraft it is likely that you are not going to be very happy, and despite this being out of the cabin crew's control, passengers will often choose to take out their anger on them.

It is the cabin crew member's responsibility in circumstances such as this to recover the situation and to make the customer happy. This could simply be by providing the high levels of customer service that you always deliver, or could be by resolving their problems or offering them some sort of compensation (if this is within your means).

✈ Manual handling
Many people will have had manual handling training in previous jobs and be familiar with the process, however for others it may be new.

As cabin crew manual handling is something that often comes into play within your role. You may have to lift a suitcase for an elderly passenger into an overhead locker, push a trolley down an aisle during turbulence or pull a container down from the top of the galley. All of these will involve manual handling.

It is very important that you undertake your job as effectively as possible and that you do not injure yourself or those around you. Legally, the airline has to provide you with training to help prevent possible injury, even if you have undertaken similar training in the past. You will be taught correct lifting techniques and techniques to push the trolley. These might sound like simple things, but if you keep making the same mistakes time and time again you could end up doing yourself some serious damage in the long run. This is why manual handling is a very important part of the cabin crew training.

✈ Equipment handling
You will also need to know how to operate and clean the equipment that you will use onboard. This will include things such as the ovens and the in flight entertainment systems. You will either be shown how to use these in a mock cabin environment or during an aircraft visit and you may be asked to demonstrate your abilities to operate various onboard equipment.

SEP Training

As cabin crew, your number one priority is the safety of your passengers. Every airline is obligated to provide a high level of SEP (safety and emergency) training. During this training you will learn a number of key topics, most of which will involve assessments. These are detailed below;

✈ Doors and exits
One of the most important roles of cabin crew is to be able to open and close the doors, especially in an emergency situation. There are several checks that you need to do before opening the door such as looking outside to check that there are no obstructions and checking that the door is in the right mode.

The doors can be put into two modes- manual or automatic. Before disembarking the crew will be instructed to put the doors into automatic, this means that in an emergency the slides will inflate upon opening the doors. The crew members will cross check each other's doors and report to the senior crew member to confirm this has been done. The same procedure will be done upon landing when the crew will put the doors back into automatic.

Different aircraft types have different doors and they are operated in different ways. As part of your training you will need to learn how to open the doors on the different aircraft you will be operating and you will need to demonstrate your ability to do this.

You will also learn about managing crown control when evacuating passengers in an emergency and the escape routes that the flight crew may use.

✈ Stages of flight
You will learn the basic physics of the theory of flight to enable you to have a general understanding. During this training you will learn what happens when the aircraft is parked on stand, during pushback, taxi, takeoff, climb, cruise, descent, approach and landing. You will also learn

about the 'point of no return', whereby the takeoff cannot be aborted under any circumstances.

✈ Flight deck door

Since the terrorist attacks of 9/11 airlines have had very strict procedures about opening and closing the flight deck door. Airlines will have procedures for opening the door (for example when taking the flight crew their meals) and you will learn what these are during your training. You will also learn the procedures for opening the door in an emergency.

Flight deck doors will normally have a code that you must enter and will have CCTV so that the flight crew can check who you are. The codes may be different for different aircraft types. You will need to learn these and will be tested on them.

✈ Unplanned emergencies

Being prepared for an emergency is your number one priority as cabin crew. Throughout your training you will be given a variety of possible scenarios and you will need to demonstrate your initiative and knowledge of relevant drills in order to pass the assessments.

In an unplanned emergency you will probably not have any time to prepare, and you will often be aware of the emergency only from the captains PA. The most common time for this is during takeoff and landing, the most dangerous times of flight. If there is an emergency, the captain will normally call the command 'this is an emergency, brace, brace'.

During your training you will learn the different brace positions for both cabin crew and passengers. You will be assessed on your knowledge of the brace positions and will need to demonstrate that you can adopt them correctly.

During your training you will also be assessed on your ability to evacuate the aircraft as quickly as possible. You will learn the drills beforehand and will need to learn these ready for your practical assessments. These will normally take place inside a mock cabin.

✈ Planned emergencies

Planned emergencies involve more procedures and drills than unplanned and therefore you will probably spend a longer period of time during your training focusing on this.

Airlines will normally have specific commands that crew will use in an emergency, this is so that you recognise the situation. You will need to learn these during your training.

As part of your training you will learn about emergency briefings and there is a common acronym (you will learn a lot of these during your training!) that is used amongst airlines. The briefing is referred to as the NITS briefing, this is when the senior crew member will give details of the Nature of the emergency, the Intention of the captain, the Time available and give and Specific instructions. You will need to learn this acronym and although you will hopefully not be using it on your flights, it is a common question that will come up during your pre-flight briefing (more about this in Chapter Three).

You will also need to learn about the different emergency equipment available to you onboard the aircraft and where they are located, again you will be tested on this. This will include items such as high visibility jackets, passenger safety cards, lifejackets (including crew, passenger, children and infant), megaphones, torches etc.

Planned emergencies could be caused by any number of things, such as an engine fire, an electrical fault or a bird strike. Although you may be just as frightened as your passengers, it is important that the crew know what they are doing and begin to undertake their drills as trained.

One of the common drills used by airlines for preparing for an emergency landing is known as the SBEA. This helps crew to remember the order that they should do things and helps to ensure that nothing is forgotten. Firstly crew must Sweep the cabin, making sure that seatbelts are fastened, tray tables are folded away, seats are upright and bags are stowed. They must then show the passengers how to adopt the Brace position, followed by demonstrating how to fasten and unfasten a

Seatbelt and showing the passengers their nearest Exit. Finally, crew need to brief their ABPs (able bodied persons).

ABPs must be people that are travelling alone so that they are willing to help others and will not be focused on their own companions, they must speak English and must be willing to help. They will be asked to hold back passengers so that the crew member can open the door and then will be the first out and will assist passengers at the bottom. They are also shown how to operate the door in the event that the crew member is unable to.

During your training you will need to demonstrate your ability to carry out the SBEA and an ABP briefing and you must pass the practical assessments. You may be given more than one try, but airlines normally limit this to only a couple of attempts.

🏃 Planned ditching

When training to become cabin crew you will need to know the procedures for ditching. A ditching is when an aircraft crash lands into the sea. Many of the same principles discussed above will apply as this may a planned or unplanned ditching.

As part of your ditching training you will need to be familiar with the different life jackets onboard. You will need to know how to operate adult and infant lifejackets as well as life cots. You will also need to know where these are stored onboard the aircraft.

The SBEA procedure discussed above will apply in exactly the same way for a planned ditching, with the addition of life jackets, meaning that it becomes LSBEA. It is the cabin crew's responsibility to ensure that passengers have located and put on their life jackets where time permits. The crew will also put on their life jackets in preparation, although crew and passengers should ensure that they do not inflate the life jackets until after they have left the aircraft as this can make evacuation difficult.

In an unplanned emergency, where crew would normally shout commands such as 'unfasten your seatbelt and come this way', they will include a reference to life jackets, for example they may shout 'unfasten your seatbelts, grab your lifejackets and come this way'. You will learn the exact commands required by your airline during your training and will be tested on this.

You will also need to learn the equipment that is available to use in the event of a ditching. Crew must learn how to use a slideraft (the usual evacuation slide has a duel use and can also be used as a raft). As part of your training you will have a swimming assessment. Some airlines, such as Emirates, have a purpose made pool, whereby the trainee crew can undertake a realistic ditching evacuation procedure. Other airlines may take their crew to a local swimming pool, within which they will be required to undertake a number of tasks.

The tasks are likely to include demonstrating that you can swim at least 25 meters and that you can tread water for a few minutes. Some airlines will ask that you wear clothes during the assessment to enable it to be as representative of a real life ditching situation as possible. You will normally be asked to demonstrate your ability to use a lifejacket and you may be asked to put one on whilst treading water in the pool. You will then need to demonstrate that you can pull yourself out of the water and into the life raft (if you don't have a lot of upper body strength, can be more difficult than you expect!). Most people pass this section of the training fine, although it is one of the parts that people worry most about! If you are not a confident swimmer it might be worth having a few lessons before commencing your training, even if just to calm your nerves!

Once you have demonstrated that you can evacuate the aircraft and climb into the raft, you need to show your knowledge of basic survival. You will learn how to use the equipment in the life raft, such as the canopy and any other emergency equipment that your airline may provide you with.

There are four priorities of survival, which are;

✈ Protection

✈ Location

✈ Water

✈ Food

During your training you will learn about survival in different conditions, such as the desert or the sea. You will learn how to keep warm, or how to keep cool. You will also learn basic principles of shelter building and lighting fires. All aircraft are fitted with ELT's (emergency locator transmitters) and you will be taught how to operate one of these. You will also be given clear instructions on staying close to the aircraft and using the survival packs that may be onboard. Purification tablets will often be kept in survival packs and you will learn how to use these, along with guidelines on eating and food.

✈ Pilot incapacitation

Pilot incapacitation can have catastrophic effects on the aircraft and passengers and it is important that the crew are able to react quickly and efficiently should such a situation occur. As part of your cabin crew training you will be taught what to do with a pilot that may be incapacitated, after all the other pilot will be busy flying the aircraft!

Airlines have specific drills for pilot incapacitation, and these will often be tested during pre-flight briefings to check that crew's knowledge is up to date. A typical pilot incapacitation drill that you will have to demonstrate is as follows;

✈ Pull incapacitated pilot upright and support

✈ Pull the seat and pilot rearwards

✈ Position the rudder pedals fully forward

🏃 Fasten the pilot's seat belt and lock the harness

🏃 Administer oxygen or first aid as required

You are likely to be tested on a pilot incapacitation drill as part of your cabin crew training.

🏃 Fire

Have you ever heard the saying 'there's no smoke without fire'? Well this could never be more important than it is onboard an aircraft. Any unusual smoke, fumes or fire must be investigated immediately by the cabin crew.

If you see smoke, many people will automatically shout 'fire!', however this is an absolute MUST NOT whilst working as cabin crew. It is important that cabin crew are specific about what they see so that the cause can be found as quickly as possible. Ever seen the footage of the Hillsborough fire in 1985? If not perhaps you should Google it.

The Hillsborough disaster demonstrated how quickly fire can spread, and many airlines will show the footage of the football stadium going up in flames so drastically to demonstrate the importance of fire onboard and aircraft, and the damage that can be caused in just a matter of minutes.

Airlines will give their cabin crew extensive training in preparation for an onboard fire. You will begin by learning the principles and chemistry of fire and the methods you can use to extinguish it. As fire is made up of the triangle of oxygen, heat and fuel, any of these components can be taken away in order to put the fire out. For example, if you take away the fuel (i.e. the wood, or whatever it is that is burning) then the fire will go out. Likewise, if you smother the fire, with say a blanket, then the oxygen will be removed and thus the fire will no longer burn. Finally, if you take away the heat of the fire by smothering it with water, the fire will be extinguished.

You will be provided with fire fighting equipment onboard the aircraft and you will need to demonstrate that you are able to use these correctly. The equipment onboard will depend on the aircraft type, but is likely to include the following;

- Fire extinguishers (sometimes known as BCF)
- Smoke hood
- Gloves
- Fire axe
- Jimmy
- Torch

Most aircraft will be equipped with BCF fire extinguishers. These are not legal on the ground in the UK, due to their high toxicity, however as they are extremely efficient they are used onboard aircraft- after all, you do not have a lot of time before an aircraft could be alight and there is no fire brigade at 30,000ft!

The smoke hood that cabin crew are instructed to use in the event of a fire may also be known as a drager. This is a breathing apparatus that you put over your head. It is made from clear plastic at the front to enable you to see and has a speech diaphragm to allow you to be able to communicate with the other crew whilst wearing the smoke hood. The smoke hood lasts a minimum of 15 minutes and should help you to breathe whilst fighting a fire onboard an aircraft. As part of your SEP training you will be required to demonstrate correct use of a smoke hood- be warned though, many crew do not like wearing them as they can make you feel rather claustrophobic. You might want to prepare yourself if this is something that may bother you as it is an essential part of the course!

During your training you will need to learn where the fire gloves are in the aircraft that you will be operating and demonstrate correct use of them. This isn't a problem for most people! You will also need to learn the location of firefighting equipment that may be onboard the aircraft such as a fire axe, jimmy and torch.

Airlines have specific drills for emergencies, and fire fighting is no different. When smoke, fire or fumes are found onboard an aircraft, three crew members are normally required to carry out the drill (if three are not available passengers may need to assist);

🛩 The firefighter

🛩 The communicator

🛩 The coordinator

The person that discovers the fire, smoke or fumes will usually be designated the firefighter. It is then their job to summon the appropriate crew members to assist and to attempt to put out the fire. The communicator is used as the point of contact between the firefighter and the flight deck and are responsible for attracting the attention of a third crew member if applicable. The third crew member will then act as the coordinator who is responsible for organising everything, from collecting the firefighting equipment for the firefighter, to clearing the area of passengers.

Once a fire has been extinguished the crew will work together to find the cause. They will also switch off any fire alarms that may be sounding. Most airlines will have very specific drills that will require the crew to learn specific statements and commands that are to be used in the event of a fire. This can be a difficult part of the training, particularly when moving between airlines as many people find it difficult to learn the procedures word for word. However, this is a very important part of the training and you will continue to be tested on these drills and commands throughout your flying career during pre-flight briefings (this will be discussed further in the Chapter Three).

Most airlines will have facilities that they use to undertake their cabin crew firefighting training, some airlines will use the facilities at local fire stations. You will learn about the different types of fires and the best ways to extinguish them. This can be an intense, but also very enjoyable part of the cabin crew training process, after all, how often do you get to extinguish a real fire without the prospect of impeding danger?

🛫 Oxygen and decompression

Aircraft are pressurised at the equivalent to the atmosphere at 5000-8000ft. This is to ensure that there is enough oxygen for us to breathe and function properly. Additionally, the cabin temperature is regulated at approximately 20 degrees Celsius, in contrast to the outside temperatures that can be as low as -55 degrees Celsius. If you have ever considered being a stow away and climbing into the hold (the undercarriage of an aircraft where the luggage and cargo is kept) then it's a good job you never have, because at such low temperatures you would not reach your destination alive!

It is important that cabin crew are trained to deal with a decompression situation, just incase such an incident should ever occur whilst they are flying. You will begin by learning about the two different types of decompression; rapid and slow.

A rapid decompression is when there is a sudden loss is pressure, for example if a window was to blow out of the aircraft. Although you will probably see this straight away, there are also a number of signs of a decompression. These include;

🛫 Pain in ears and sinuses
🛫 Mist in the cabin
🛫 Sudden drop in temperature
🛫 The appearance of the drop down oxygen masks in the cabin
🛫 Sudden boiling of liquids
🛫 Smoke detectors may activate
🛫 The cabin air becoming thin and cold

In the event of a rapid decompression you will be trained to take the nearest oxygen mask and to put it on. You will then sit down and hold on tightly wherever you can, even if this means sitting on a passenger! There are different oxygen systems that can be used onboard an aircraft and you will learn how they operate. Once it is safe you will need to transfer to your portable oxygen, this may be located near your crew seat. This may mean that you will need to swing, almost 'monkey like' from one oxygen mask to the next through the cabin until you reach the portable oxygen. There are additional drop down oxygen masks on each row so this should be relatively practical to do.

During your training you will also learn about slow decompressions, and how to recognise these. A slow decompression is far less obvious than a rapid decompression and could be caused by very small gaps in windows or doors etc. When experiencing a slow decompression, crew and passengers are likely to begin to feel tired and disorientated. Crew will often notice this first as they are undertaking more physical activities than the passengers, who may be sat still or asleep. Crew may find it difficult to push the trolley or to lift items that do not usually feel heavy to them. Crew and passengers can start to become quite confused and may not be able to identify that the cause is a result of a reduction in the cabin air pressure. If you suspect a slow decompression, it is important to communicate with the flight crew so that they can investigate it.

✈ Safety demonstration

When you think of cabin crew, the safety demo is perhaps the first thing that comes to mind. Whether you pay attention or not, this is a very important part of a cabin crew member's job role and is compulsory under the CAA regulations. Some airlines now use a video to convey the relevant information, whereas others ask their cabin crew to undertake a full manual safety demo on each and every flight.

The safety demo consists of a number of safety aspects that are important for passengers to be aware of should there be an accident or incident onboard. Each airline will have their own spiel, although they will all cover the same content, which consists of;

✈ Safety card

Crew (or a pre-prepared video) will demonstrate what the safety card is and where it is located. They will also point out the instructions of how to undertake the brace position.

Nearest exit

Cabin crew will point out your nearest exit. Whether a video is used or the crew are undertaking a manual demonstration, they will also point out the exits. Crew will be positioned throughout the aircraft so that every passenger can see a crew member.

Aisle lighting

In the case of an emergency, emergency lighting will illuminate along the aisles to help passengers see where they are going. The crew will point this out.

Seatbelt

It is important that all passengers are aware of how to buckle and unbuckle their seatbelt. During an emergency there may not be time to struggle with seatbelts so the cabin crew, or the video if used, will demonstrate the correct use.

Lifejacket

Cabin crew will demonstrate how to put on a lifejacket and the different functions that it has, such as a torch, whistle and inflation tube. They will also show the passengers where these can be located. The lifejackets used on airlines will differ slightly. Some airlines may not even use lifejackets, for example Spice Jet, an Indian low cost airline, use their seat cushions as 'flotation devices' in an emergency ditching situation!

Oxygen mask

The cabin crew, or video, will demonstrate how to use the oxygen masks in the event of a decompression.

You probably won't spend too much time focusing on the flight demo during your training, as this is an art you will have time to perfect when you are out online, but you will normally be introduced to it.

⇗Dangerous goods

As part of your cabin crew training you will learn some of the things that you should look out for when flying. Some airlines will bring in professionals that work within safety and security to teach you.

For instance, BA City Flyer has been known to use members of the police force to come in and train their cabin crew. They show crew a number of different items, of which would probably not stand out to the average person whatsoever. They then explain how a group of terrorists could carry a couple of items each and how these can then be put together to form a gun!

It is also important for crew to understand the reasons behind some of the health and safety restrictions that are in place. For instance, why do you have to take your shoes off at security these days? Well this is all due to the infamous shoe bomber. In 2001, a man named Richard Reid packed explosives into his shoes and boarded flight 63 from Paris to Miami. Fortunately Richard, a member of Al Qaeda, failed to detonate the explosives and was subdued by passengers. The aircraft then diverted to Boston, the nearest airport, and Richard was later sentenced to life in prison. It is because of this incident that you will now often have your shoes checked at airport security.

What about the flight deck door, why can't we take our children in there any more to meet the pilot? Well this is a direct result of September 11. During the 9/11 terrorist attacks, the flight deck was intruded by terrorists, who then went on to take control of the aircraft, crash into the twin towers in New York and cause huge devastation and loss of life. This is the worst incident of terrorism in the air to date. In response to this tragic event, all airlines now operate a strict locked door policy. This means that the only people that can enter the cockpit are the cabin crew, and even this is under strict procedures.

You will learn about how to deal with bombs during your training. There is a least risk bomb location on an aircraft (usually at the back) and crew will be given training on how to move the bomb and cover it with materials that will reduce the impact on explosion, such as seat cushions and passenger cabin luggage.

• • •

🛩 Passenger restraint

Cabin crew training covers much more than most people will imagine, and one of the more unusual things that you will do is restraint training. There are no emergency services at 30,000ft, so if there is an unruly or particularly difficult passenger that is risking the safety of others onboard, it is the crew's responsibility to resolve the situation. Your restraint training will include learning how to use handcuffs sufficiently and practicing restraining a person to an aircraft seat using the restraint kits that most aircraft will have onboard. Although this is obviously a very important area of the training, it can also be really good fun!

🛩 Crew resource management

CRM is an integral part of the cabin crew training process and can be defined as an effective use of all resources, physical or otherwise, to achieve safe and efficient flight operations. Statistics have shown that three quarters of aircraft accidents are as a result of human error, and thus CRM can help to minimise this. Have you ever watched Air Crash Investigation? If it doesn't put you off flying, it will demonstrate to you how accidents can often occur as a result of human error and the importance of good team work and communication onboard.

🛩 Aircraft security checks

Security checks are extremely important and it is the cabin crew's responsibility to undertake these before every flight. You will learn about the different checks and why they are important during your training. Crew members will often be given individual responsibilities to undertake. For instance, the number ten crew member may be responsible for checking the OHAR, whereas the number three may be responsible for checking the fire alarms. Each crew member will also check the emergency equipment in the vicinity of their crew seat.

Cabin crew will have routine checks that they will carry out throughout the flight, such as checking the toilets. It is also their job to monitor any suspicious looking passengers or unusual behavior and report this to the flight deck.

Avmed Training

Avmed stands for aviation medicine and is an extremely important part of your training. If there is a medical incident you may well be the most qualified person to deal with it, and so airlines give you training on a range of possible medical incidents that could occur onboard an aircraft. This will be a challenging part of your training as it will consist of a range of practical and written assessments, but it can also be very useful whether you are at 30,000ft or whether you have your feet firmly on the ground! Your training will consist of a number of different aspects, of which are outlined below;

✈ Effects of flying on the body

Not only do you need to be able to assist your passengers in a medical situation, but you also need to be able to look after yourself, and in doing so it is important that you understand the effects that flying may have on your body.

The pressurised cabin can make you tire out more quickly than normal and cause alcohol to have greater effects on the body. It is said that two hours work on the ground is the equivalent to one hour in the air... and people think working as cabin crew is easy! Likewise, it is also said that one alcoholic drink in the air can equate to two drinks on the ground, although you probably won't be drinking whilst working as crew, you will most likely be serving drinks so it is important to be aware of this.

Working as cabin crew can be a very demanding job and can play havoc with your routine and your eating and sleeping patterns. Did you know that the average Club Class meal for British Airways contains roughly 2000 calories? That's the recommended calorie intake for a woman for an entire day! So be warned, onboard food may not be the healthiest for you and many crew choose to take their own food with them.

Establishing a regular sleeping pattern is virtually impossible whilst working as cabin crew. Don't like early mornings or late nights? Then working as cabin crew may not be the job for you. From 4am starts, to midnight finishes, to night flights, your body will find adjusting difficult at times. Onboard the larger aircraft you will probably have crew rest facilities so that you can have a sleep during your break, but for many switching on and off like a light bulb isn't easy. During your training you will be taught about the importance of sleep and sleep cycles and many crew will live by these in order to manage their sleep patterns!

✈ Travel health
In preparation for your flying career it is likely that you will need to have some vaccinations. You will also be required to undertake disinsection when flying in and out of certain destinations. When flying to Malaria areas you will need to take deet with you, this is used to repel the mosquitoes and your airline will normally provide you with this. You will not usually take Malaria tablets as these are not good for your health when taken on a long term basis, and as you are likely to be flying to such areas often you would quite likely be taking the tablets most of your flying career!

During your training you will learn about monitoring travel health and how to spot any obvious infectious diseases or illnesses that could impact on the health of passengers onboard.

✈ CPR
Cardiopulmonary resuscitation, commonly known as CPR is an important skill that trainee crew will need to learn. There are a number of reasons that CPR could be necessary onboard an aircraft and you will need to demonstrate your competency in doing so. This will usually be in the form of a practical assessment.

You will learn about conducting a primary survey and will be assessed on your abilities to check for danger, check the casualties response, send for help, check their airways, check their breathing and then to administer CPR or defibrillation as necessary. You will also need to demonstrate that you can undertake a secondary survey. This generally consists of finding out relevant information about the condition from the casualty and could include questions such as 'have you experienced this before?', 'are you taking any medication?' and 'How long has this been happening?'.

You will need to demonstrate during your training that you can put a passenger in the recovery position, open and clear their airways and check their breathing and pulse. You will learn the correct procedure for administering CPR and will need to demonstrate your ability to do this for babies, infants and adults. You will also learn how to use the defibrillator (also known as the defib).

⚒ Medical emergencies
There are a huge range of medical emergencies that could occur onboard an aircraft. Should there be an emergency the first thing to do is to contact the flight crew who will decide whether they should divert. However diverting is not always possible, and in this case you will have to be the emergency medic. Airlines will have radio contact with MedLink who can advise you on what you should do and you may call for a doctor if needed, although there are no guarantees that there will be one onboard!

Medical emergencies can be very scary and crew are trained to deal with a wide range of potential situations. You will be tested on each of the following demonstrating your knowledge to identify the medical condition and administer first aid or medical assistance where possible;

⚒ Choking
⚒ Asthma attacks
⚒ Hyperventilation
⚒ Angina
⚒ Heart attack
⚒ Fainting
⚒ DVT (deep vein thrombosis)
⚒ Hypovolemic shock
⚒ Nausea and vomiting
⚒ Diarrhea
⚒ Abdominal pain
⚒ Headache
⚒ Ingestion and heartburn
⚒ Bleeding
⚒ Motion sickness
⚒ Urinary retention

- Fits or convulsions
- Stroke
- Panic attack
- Alcohol intoxication
- Diabetes
- Hypoglycemia
- Hyperglycemia
- Anaphylaxis
- Allergy
- Ear and sinus pain
- Nosebleed
- Eye irritation
- Decompression sickness
- Sickle cell anemia

Alongside the comprehensive list above you will also learn about pregnancy and childbirth, did you know that cabin crew are also midwives in need be? As cabin crew you need to be prepared for any situation onboard, and child birth is one of them! You will learn about delivering the baby, cutting the umbilical cord and delivering the placenta. A bit squeamish? If you want to be cabin crew you might need to get over that before commencing your training!

- Trauma emergencies

Alongside medical emergencies, you will be trained and assessed on how to deal with trauma situations. These include;

- Cuts and grazes
- Severe bleeding
- Amputation
- Chest injuries
- Abdominal injuries
- Fractures
- Tying a sling
- Strains and sprains
- Leg, knee and foot injuries
- Head injuries
- Neck and back injuries

⚔ Burns or scalds
⚔ Smoke inhalation
⚔ Electrical injuries
⚔ Frostbite
⚔ Hypothermia
⚔ Heat exhaustion
⚔ Heatstroke
⚔ Injuries to the eye

In order to carry out the medical assistance that a passenger may need, you are provided with a range of first aid equipment onboard the aircraft. As part of your training you will learn about the defib and the different first aid boxes available to you, where these are located, what is for your use and what is for medical professionals. You will also learn about the documentation that needs to be completed when administering first aid.

Thought Avmed training was just about CPR and your usual basic first aid? Think again!

Aircraft Types

When working as cabin crew you could be working on a number of different aircraft. CAA regulations state that this should be a maximum of three, however there can be different variations of the same aircraft. This regulation is in place to ensure optimum safety for the passengers; after all, most people would struggle to remember all the details of every aircraft!

During your training you will be taken on an aircraft visit, whereby you are able to familiarise yourself with the aircraft that you will be working on. The rest of your training will be in mock cabins. You will need to learn many things about the aircraft such as equipment location, codes to use for the phone and procedures for opening the doors. This is a particularly tough part of the training for many people as there is a lot to remember!

Most airlines will use Boeing or Airbus aircraft, although some will also use other aircraft types such as the Embraer or the Avro RJ. Below is a summary of some of the common aircraft that you may work on as cabin crew-

✈ Airbus A319/20/21

These three aircraft are all variations of the same plane, and as such airlines can get away with asking you to operate as all three but only classifying it as one. This can get particularly confusing for trainee crew as there are many subtle differences between the aircraft that you will need to remember.

These airbus aircraft are generally used for short haul routes and are commonly used by a number of airlines including British Airways, easyJet and Ryan Air.

✈ Airbus 340

This is a larger aircraft and is also used by a number of airlines on predominantly long haul routes. All crew that work for Virgin Atlantic will need to familiarise themselves with this aircraft type.

✈ Airbus A380

Some call it the queen of this skies, this is the largest aircraft in operation and the world's first double decker aeroplane. Many airlines have now invested in A380's as the newest additions to their fleet including British Airways, Qantas and Emirates. An airbus A380 can seat a maximum of 853 passengers and requires more onboard crew than any other aircraft. They will usually operate on longhaul routes.

✈ Boeing 777

This is a popular longhaul aircraft that is used by many airlines. This aircraft type also has different variations that crew may need to familiarise themselves with.

✈ Boeing 747

This is many people's favourite aircraft. The traditional jumbo jet has been in operation since 1970 and is a very popular aircraft used by airlines on their longhaul routes.

✈ Boeing 787 Dreamliner

This is a new aircraft type that many airlines have recently chosen to purchase for their fleets. It can seat up to 335 passengers and is predominantly used for longhaul routes.

As part of your cabin crew training you will need to demonstrate a thorough knowledge of the aircraft types that you will be working on. This is likely to include a series of exams and lots of revision. You may need to complete location diagrams, showing that you know where all of the equipment you may use as cabin crew is located onboard.

Passing the Training Course

Your initial training will consist of a number of assessments. Some of these will be exam or test based, others will be practical assessments. Each airline will have its own specific requirements, however they are all obligated to ensure that you are qualified to the required standard in order to ensure the safety and security if passengers onboard. As such, unfortunately there are often cabin crew that are not successful in passing their initial training and that do not ever make it to their dream job in the skies.

Each airline will have its own procedures for monitoring and assessing the suitability of trainee crew. Some airlines may use a points system or hand out snapshots when crew do not satisfactorily perform for instance. They will have a limit of how many points or snapshots a person can accrue before they are asked to leave the course.

There are many things that can cause a person to accrue points or snapshots, and as such below are things for you to watch out for on your training course!

✈ Uniform standards

Uniform standards are VERY important to airlines. If you can't demonstrate that you can adhere to them during your training then how do they know you will adhere to them once you are online? They don't! Many crew have been awarded points or snapshots for things such as creases in their shirts, their hair not being neat enough or for not reapplying their lipstick!

Making sure your uniform looks good is a simple task- don't get awarded negative marks for not getting it right!

✈ Punctuality

Punctuality is integral to the successful operation of any airline, and as such it is very important that crew are on time to work, after all, if the crew aren't there then the flight can not leave!

During your training course the trainers will be monitoring your punctuality and it has been known for crew to be asked to leave the airline for being late to work (although they will normally give you more than one chance). Airlines will be very strict on lateness throughout your employment, so start as you mean to go on- do not be late!

✈ Assessments

Not passing assessments is probably the biggest reason that somebody might be given negative marks, and could be the reason for your dismissal. The biggest advice here is revise, revise, revise! They do not say the training course is the toughest thing you will do as cabin crew for nothing! You will have a lot to take in and you will learn a lot of new things. Don't expect to have a social life during your training course because you will spend your evenings and weekends revising! Work hard and it will pay off eventually!

Supernumerary Flight

Upon completion of your training course you will be given your first roster which will include a supernumerary flight. This is your first working flight where you will act as an extra crew member. It is your chance to familiarise yourself with onboard services and security practices and to ask any questions you may have. You are also often given the opportunity to work in the different cabins and even experience take off or landing from the flight deck!

Airline Terminology

Becoming a part of the aviation industry can be a daunting experience....because there are so many new terms and words that you will need to learn! Below is a description of some of the new terminology that you will need to familarise yourself with;

- **ABP**- Able bodied person. This is a person that will be used to assist in an emergency situation onboard the aircraft. They must be travelling alone, willing to help and be able to speak Engish.
- **AD**- this stands for assessment day. This is a day where you will be assessed for your suitability as cabin crew and will include a formal interview as well as a number of activities/ tasks/ tests.
- **Allowances**- This is the money allocated to crew whilst they are downroute.
- **Approach**- this is when the aircraft is coming in to land, it is one of the final stages of flight.
- **Apron**- The area of the airport where aircraft are parked, unloaded or loaded, refueled or boarded.
- **ATC**- This is an abbreviation for air traffic control, the people that watch over and command movement of air traffic.
- **Avmed**- This is the term used to describe aviation medicine. This will cover a range of first aid and medical assistance that crew are trained to administer.
- **Base**- Cabin crew will always work from a base, this is their main airport that they will fly in and out of. Sometimes crew may be duel based and may have more than one.
- **Boarding**- The time when passengers get on the aircraft.
- **Brace**- This is the position to be adopted upon an emergency landing. Brace positions differ for crew and passengers. Passengers will be familiar with the brace position for the safety demonstration and the safety card found in their seat pocket.
- **Budget airline**- Also known as a low cost carrier or a no frills airline these are airlines that offer few luxuries onboard in return for cheap prices.
- **CAA**- Civil Aviation Authority. This is the governing body that sets many of the rules and regulations that airlines and crew must abide by.

Cabin- The area of the aircraft where passengers are seated. There may be different classes of cabin such as first class or economy.

Cabin sweep- This is when the cabin crew member walks through the cabin ensuring that all passengers are ready for landing. They will check seatbelts on are, tray tables are up, seats are upright and all bags are adequately stowed.

Charter airline- An airline that does not run to a schedule. Flights can be operated on an ad-hoc basis and are often associated with package holidays.

Circle- This is when the aircraft is required to wait until they can land, usually as a result of heavy air traffic and common in busy airports such as London Heathrow. They will often 'circle' the airport until they are allowed to land.

Commission- This is the money that cabin crew are paid when they sell onboard products. It is usually a percentage of the amount sold.

CRB- This stands for criminal record bureau and is a criminal record check that every cabin crew member must pass in order to obtain their airport ID.

Crew purchase- Heavily discounted alcohol that cabin crew can buy whilst on the aircraft.

Crew rest- This is the area that is dedicated to crew found onboard some aircraft types. It may have seats or beds.

Cruise- This is the main part of the flight, whereby the pilots are simply following the pre-determined flight path. This is the time when they can eat and have their crew rest.

Day light saving time- the practice of advancing standard time by one hour in the spring of each year and of setting it back by one hour in the fall in order to gain an extra period of daylight during the early evening.

Deet- A product used to prevent mosquito bites, often provided by airlines when crew are flying to areas with a high risk of Malaria.

Defib- This is short for defibrillator, the piece of equipment used to re-start a person's heart during a medical emergency.

Disembarkation- The process of passengers leaving the aircraft

Disinsection- When the cabin crew spray the cabin with chemicals to prevent insects from contaminating the aircraft. This only occurs in certain risk destinations.

Ditching- An emergency landing into water.

Down route- The time when crew are way from base before their return flight home.

Duty free- Goods that can be purchased onboard an aircraft or at the airport without incurring any taxes.

DVT- this stands for Deep Vein Thrombosis. This is a condition that results from blood clots forming in the veins that can occur when onboard a long haul flight.

ELT- This stands for emergency locator transmitter and is used onboard an aircraft to locate it in the event of an emergency.

FDP- This stands for flight duty pay. This is the money that crew may be given for the hours that they fly. This is not used by every airline.

Flight crew- The pilots.

Flight deck- The area in which the pilots sit.

Flight path- The pre-determined route that the aircraft will fly.

Float- The bag of change carried by a crew member.

Galley- This is the area that is used by the cabin crew to prepare meals etc. It is usually situated at the front and rear and between cabins, although this differs between aircraft types.

Gash- A bizarre word crew use for rubbish!

Gillet- A sleeveless garment often worn over a shirt during the cabin service.

GMT- This stands for Greenwich Mean Time and is the time zone in which cabin crew rosters are normally written.

High vis- This is short for high visibility jacket. Crew will wear this during emergency evacuations and when in potentially dangerous areas such as when walking from the terminal building across the apron to the aircraft.

Hold- The area in the undercarriage of the aircraft where the cargo and passenger luggage are kept.

Jump seat- The foldable seat in the galley or cabin that crew sit on during take off and landing.

Manifest- The list of passengers onboard the aircraft and any special requirements. Also known as a passenger list.

MedLink- A telephone service between flight crew and medical assistance on the ground.

Nightstop- When cabin crew spend a night away from base. Also known as a stopover.

Longhaul- This is generally a flight that is over six hours in duration.

OHAR- Overhead crew rest area. This is the area dedicated to crew rest that is located above the passengers. There will be stairs to access this area. This is not found on all aircraft types.

Online- When you are working for the airline as an operating cabin crew after you have passed your initial cabin crew training.

PA- This stands for personal announcement. These are the announcements made during the flight by the cabin or flight crew.

Passenger load- The number of passengers onboard the flight or in a particular cabin.

PAX- The code used for the term passengers.

Purser- A senior crew member.

Pushback- The moment when the aircraft is pushed away from the apron area towards the runway.

Red notice- An update to the printed manuals.

Roster- The timetable given to crew to outline their duties for the month

Scheduled airline- An airline that runs to a schedule. National carriers are usually examples of scheduled airlines.

SEP- Safety and emergency procedures. This is essential training that crew must undertake.

Sector- One leg of the journey.

Shorthaul- This is generally a flight that is under six hours in duration.

Stand- The place where the aircraft is parked.

Standby- When a crew member or aircraft is asked to literally 'stand by' until they are called for a flight. Crew can undertake this at home, known as 'home standby' or at the airport, known as 'airport standby'.

Stowed- when an item is securely put away.

Supernumerary flight- This is when you work as an extra crew member onboard an aircraft, usually as your first familiarisation flight.

✈ **Taxi**- This is the time that the aircraft moves from its stand to the runway.

✈ **Tech**- This is short for technical and is the term used when an aircraft is out of operation due to a technical problem.

✈ **There and back**- A shift that includes flying to a destination and back without a stopover.

✈ **Turnaround**- The time between landing and take off again.

✈ **Working position**- The position that the crew member is asked to work during the flight. This is usually a number ranking with the most senior being number one.

Passenger Codes

There are also a number of different codes that you need to learn as cabin crew. Below is a summary of some of the key terms that you may come across;

Meal codes (you will need to know these when delivering the service onboard the aircraft);

✈ AVML- Asian vegetarian meal
✈ BBML- Infant/ baby meal
✈ CHML- Child meal
✈ DBML- Diabetic meal
✈ FPML- Fruit platter
✈ GFML- Gluten free meal
✈ HNML- Hindu (non vegetarian) meal
✈ KSML- Kosher meal
✈ LCML- Low calorie meal
✈ LFML- low fat/ low cholesterol meal
✈ LSML- Low sodium/ salt meal
✈ MOML- Muslim meal
✈ NLML- Non lactose meal
✈ ORML- Oriental meal
✈ SFML- Sea food meal
✈ SPML- Special meal, food to be specified
✈ VGML- vegetarian meal

Passengers with reduced mobility codes (you will need to know these during boarding and when reading the passenger list/ manifest);

- ✈ WCHR- A passenger who requires a wheelchair or other means for movements between the aircraft and the terminal, in the terminal and between arrival and departure points on the city side of the terminal.
- ✈ WCHS- A passenger who cannot walk up or down stairs, but who can move about in an aircraft cabin and requires a wheelchair to move between the aircraft, in the terminal and between arrival and departure points on the city side of the terminal.
- ✈ WCHP- A passenger who requires assistance to embark or disembark and who can move about in an aircraft cabin only with the help of an on- board wheelchair.
- ✈ WCHC- A passenger who is completely immobile who can move about only with the help of a wheelchair or any other means and who requires assistance at all times from arrival at the airport to seating in the aircraft, or if necessary, in a special seat fitted to his/her specific needs the process being inverted at arrival.
- ✈ BLND- A blind passenger.
- ✈ DEAF- A passenger who is deaf or a passenger who is deaf without speech.
- ✈ UNMIN- An unaccompanied minor.

Airport Codes

When you receive your first roster you may well be very confused as everything is written in 'airline speak'. All of the destinations can be identified by the airport code shown on your roster. Code such as MAN (Manchester) or EDI (Edinburgh) may be relatively easy to work out, but there are also many codes such as GIG (Rio De Janeiro) that are far less obvious! Below is a list of some of the airport codes that you may come across when flying, although there are many, many more for you to remember!

- ✈ LHR- London Heathrow
- ✈ MAN- Manchester
- ✈ LGW- London Gatwick
- ✈ EDI- Edinburgh
- ✈ GLA- Glasgow
- ✈ LTN- London Luton
- ✈ STN- London Stansted
- ✈ AMS- Amsterdam
- ✈ CDG- Paris Charles De Gaulle
- ✈ MUC- Munich
- ✈ BCN- Barcelona
- ✈ MAD- Madrid
- ✈ PRG- Prague
- ✈ HEL- Helsinki
- ✈ NCE- Nice
- ✈ HAM- Hamburg
- ✈ ATH- Athens
- ✈ RKV- Reykjavik
- ✈ FCO- Rome
- ✈ OSL- Oslo
- ✈ KRK- Krakow
- ✈ WAW- Warsaw
- ✈ FAO- Faro
- ✈ IST- Istanbul
- ✈ BNK- Bangkok
- ✈ HKG- Hong Kong
- ✈ KUL- Kula Lumpa
- ✈ SIN- Singapore
- ✈ DEL- Delhi
- ✈ CPT- Cape Town
- ✈ LOS- Lagos
- ✈ SYD- Sydney
- ✈ MEL- Melbourne
- ✈ CHC- Christchurch
- ✈ BAI- Buenos Aires
- ✈ GIG- Rio De Janeiro
- ✈ MEX- Mexico City
- ✈ JFK- New York JFK

- ✈ SFO- San Francisco
- ✈ LAS- Las Vegas
- ✈ LAX- Los Angeles
- ✈ YOW- Ottawa Macdonald-Cartier
- ✈ DEN- Denver
- ✈ NRT- Tokyo Narita
- ✈ PEK- Beijing
- ✈ DXB- Dubai

Airline Codes

Alongside codes for different airports, each airline will also have their own code. This is how you can identify the airline operating the flight simply from reading the associated code or flight number. Some examples include;

- ✈ BA- British Airways
- ✈ VS- Virgin Atlantic
- ✈ EZY- easyJet
- ✈ EK- Emirates
- ✈ AA- American Airlines
- ✈ IB- Iberia
- ✈ SQ- Singapore Airlines
- ✈ SR- Swiss Air
- ✈ TG- Thai Airways
- ✈ QF- Qantas
- ✈ AY- Finnair
- ✈ AF- Air France

Chapter Three: Life in The Skies

Working as Cabin Crew

Working as cabin crew is certainly a unique job, and as a result there are often many unanswered questions about what it is like to work at 30,000ft. This chapter explains what you will be doing whilst working as cabin crew and aims to answer many of your pre-start date questions that you may have.

Money

Upon commencing your career as cabin crew you are bound to have a million and one questions, some of the most important perhaps regarding money. Most people do not choose to become cabin crew because of the lucrative salary on offer (or not as the case may be), but they often choose it for their love of customer service and travel. However, it is money that makes the world go round and it is important that you manage your finances sufficiently.

✈ Wages

Some airlines provide very competitive packages for their crew and a prime example is Emirates. Secure a job with this airline and they will pay you a competitive salary of around £2000 a month (tax free), provide you with a free apartment for you to live in and offer you numerous discounts on travel, local businesses etc. However, they do require you to live in Dubai. This may be an added bonus for some people, but for others it may be a deal breaker.

Unfortunately however, many airlines are not as competitive as the likes of Emirates. Competition to become cabin crew can be extremely high, and as such airlines can afford to pay their crew relatively low salaries as they rarely struggle to recruit. A good example of an airline who's salaries have been under scrutiny recently is British Airways. Traditionally, they operated through two fleets; Worldwide and Eurofleet. The crew working for these fleets were paid very good salaries, and over the years there were a number of negotiations through the unions and their salaries continued to increase. Their salaries increased so much so that many of the crew, who are now dependent on the money they take home each month, struggle to move between airlines or to change careers, as an alternative occupation would often not pay as much as they earn working for BA.

BA were paying some crew salaries so high that they were in fact earning more than some of the pilots! This was clearly an unsustainable situation for the airline, particularly when faced with issues such as rising fuel costs and increased competition from low cost carriers. In response, BA created a new fleet, known as Mixed Fleet. From this time on all new staff have been recruited onto the new fleet, on new terms on conditions, causing the two old fleets to gradually reduce in size. Mixed Fleet offers significantly lower salaries and more stringent working conditions than the previous fleets.

BA claim that their salaries are in line with other carriers employment packages, and if you are worked to full capacity (i.e. given a full roster each month) you may well earn the same as you would for easyJet, Thomas Cook or Virgin Atlantic. However, you cannot guarantee your roster, nor your monthly take home. BA cabin crew wages start at £12,000 per annum, not including flight pay and allowances.

In general though, basic cabin crew salaries range from approximately £12,000- £20,000 a year. However many crew will take home more than this through allowances and commission.

✈ Commission
Many cabin crew members will make much of their money through commission. This is when cabin crew sell onboard products and are then rewarded by earning a percentage of the money made. Although this can be a big money earner, it is more prominent in some airlines over others. For instance, low cost carriers such as easyJet place a big emphasis on selling as this is how the airline makes much of its profit. This means then that the crew are likely to sell far more onboard products and thus earn more commission than some of the competing airlines. Scheduled airlines, for instance, tend to provide passengers with meals and drinks free of charge, they also place far lesser emphasis on purchasing duty free, as a result the crew sell less products and make less commission.

✈ Allowances

Although scheduled airlines may not offer crew as many opportunities to earn high commission as the low cost airlines, they do often provide crew will allowances for their time down route. This comes in different shapes and forms depending on the airline that you choose to work for. Some airlines, such as Virgin Atlantic, provide crew with a card, upon which money is allocated for the crew member to use whilst down route. The money given will depend on the destination visited and the cost of living there. For instance, two nights in Lagos in Nigeria will earn crew substantially less than two nights in Los Angeles as a result of the differences in the cost of living. Other airlines may choose to provide crew with an hourly paid allowance, for example British Airways give their crew flight duty pay, known as FDP. When working for BA's Mixed fleet you will be given an hourly paid rate (at the time of writing this was set at £2.80) and you are awarded this from the moment you check in until the moment you check out. As such if you were to work a six hour there and back you would only earn additional £16.80 on top of your salary, whereas 5 days in Rio may earn you up to an extra £330!

✈ Staff benefits

Cabin crew salaries differ greatly between airlines and can be relatively low, however there are many benefits that you are likely to receive. These are airline dependent, but some typical examples are listed below;

✈ Free flights

✈ Flight upgrades

✈ Discounted flights for you and your friends and family

✈ High class accommodation provided whilst down route

✈ Free crew meals onboard the aircraft

✈ Free meals down route

✈ Discounted entrance fees to major tourist attractions

✈ Discounted car hire rental

✈ Discounts on high street hotels

✈ Discounts on phone rental packages

✈ Discounts in high street retailers such as the Apple store

✈ Free uniforms

✈ Free cabin crew training

✈ Discounted gym memberships

✈ Free apartment (when based overseas)

✈ Tax free allowances (such as FDP)

As you can see there are certainly a wide range of perks to working as cabin crew and it can often be one of the reasons people choose the job!

✈ Living costs

When working as cabin crew you will need to carefully assess your living situation, as life in the skies is very different from a 9-5 job. For instance, many crew choose to commute; some people travel across the country and some may even travel internationally to get to work! Working as cabin crew can bring opportunities that you may never have had before, for example with heavily discounted flights you can jump on a plane to work just as easily as you could a bus! Your ability to commute long distances to work will obviously depend on your roster, but for many it is a popular choice of living that allows you to travel the world, without ever leaving home for more than a few days.

Other people may choose to relocate near to the airport. This can make life easier as you will not have the stress of long distance travel to and from work, however it can also be costly and lonely. Many crew will choose to rent a room and depending on the airport you are based at this can cost a small fortune. If you choose to live near London Heathrow for example you are likely to end up paying in excess of £500 a month (unless you are living in one of the undesirable areas such as Slough or Hounslow of which many crew would not touch with a barge pole!). Living near the airport might be easier, but it can also be frustrating when you are contributing towards the costs of bills etc even though you are away more often than you are home! Many people choose to rent a house with their colleagues, and although this can be fun at times, in reality it is unlikely that there will be many occasions that your rosters marry up to allow you to spend time at home together. As a result you are likely to end up spending a lot of time home alone.

There are also 'crew rooms' and hotels available. Although this is obviously not a long term solution, many crew will choose to stay near the airport when their roster dictates that commuting will not be worthwhile, for example if finishing late one evening and then starting early again the next morning. Crew rooms and budget hotels can cost as little as around £20 per night surrounding London Heathrow and less at smaller UK airports.

However, depending on the airline you are applying to, you may not need to worry about living circumstances. If you choose to work for Emirates for example, you will be provided with an apartment in Dubai that you will share with other crew members. This can be lonely, as crew will be working to different rosters and you can also be home alone. You are also likely to be away from your friends and family. Moving away for work is a big commitment, some love it and others do not. If you are interested in working for the likes of Emirates, make sure that you do your research first to ensure that it is the best airline for you!

Whilst working as cabin crew that are plenty of ways of reducing your living costs such as staying in crew rooms and commuting from home when appropriate (if you live with your parents or will save money on rent/ mortgage by living away from the airport). You can also use your discounts (airline dependent) that can get you things such as cheaper line rental on your phone contracts and international calling and data packages, cheap flights etc. Working as cabin crew may not be the highest paid job in the world, but it does have a lot of perks as discussed above, and if you manage your money correctly you can get along very well financially.

Rosters

All cabin crew work to a roster. This is effectively a timetable, outlining your shifts for the month/week. You will normally be notified of your roster a few days before it begins.

Rosters are subject to change at any time, and this can make planning a social life rather difficult! Your airline will ask you to regularly check your roster for changes and these will be highlighted to you. For instance, you could return home from a trip to find that instead of working a Madrid there and back the next day, you have been changed to a five day Tokyo trip! The airline industry is dynamic and ever changing, and this is certainly represented within a cabin crew member's roster!

Your roster will normally be written in GMT (Greenwich Mean Time) and does not account for day light saving time- which can become rather confusing when reading your roster! Your roster will be written using the 24 hour clock. It will be written using the airline codes discussed in Chapter Two, and although it is important that you do learn these eventually, it is not uncommon for crew to 'Google' the code upon receiving their roster to find out where they will be going in the early days of their crew life!

Rosters can look very confusing, but as crew you will soon learn how to read them accurately. Depending on the airline you work for you may have a variety of flights on your roster. Qantas Heathrow based crew for example, currently predominantly operate the LHR-DXB-LHR route, so their roster would be dominated by flights to Dubai. In contrast, British Airways Mixed fleet fly to a large range of both short haul and long haul destinations, so their rosters could be completely different each month, in fact, you could fly for a year without visiting every destination!
    ✈ Bidding

Some crew prefer particular destinations/ routes/ flying times over others, and as such many airlines will do their best to meet the needs and preferences of their cabin crew where business needs allow. Many airlines will offer some form of bidding or swap system, whereby crew can put in their preferences. Crew may be able to specify that they want to avoid early starts or that they do not want to visit particular destinations. They can also put in a preference for destinations that they would like to visit and days that they would like off. Although in theory a bidding system is a great idea, it can be difficult to give crew everything they want, and therefore there is no guarantee that crew will get what they ask for. If this is the case, many airlines will allow crew to swap shifts where possible. Many crew set up websites or Facebook pages to discuss the swapping of flights.

✈ Standby

Within your roster you are likely to have some standby shifts. This is literally what it says on the box- you 'stand by' until you are needed. There are generally two types of standby, home standby and airport standby. When at home you are free to do what you want until you are called, but you will usually be given a minimum time until you must report for duty. This can sometimes be a requirement by the airline when hiring crew as they will often dictate that the prospective cabin crew member must live within 60-90 minutes of the airport (although many crew will simply book a hotel room for standby duties such as this if they live further away). Airport standby is when a crew member must wait at the airport until they are called. This can be very boring and tedious and is often not very popular with crew!

When on a standby duty you need to be prepared to operate any flight and you may need to have a bag packed in preparation. You will need to pack for every eventuality; could you be going to a snowy Nepal or a baking hot Las Vegas? Then you'll need to pack your snow boots along with your bikini! Standby shifts can be stressful as you don't know where you might be sleeping that night, but they can also be quite exciting as you wait in anticipation to find out what destination you may be jetting off to next!

Pre Flight Briefings

When you report for duty you will begin by checking in and checking for any red notices (amendments to the manuals). You will then do any administrative duties that you may need to do before reporting for your pre-flight briefing.

Pre-flight briefings are often the most stressful part of a cabin crew member's day. Hate tests? Hate being put on the spot? Have a bad memory? Then working as cabin crew may not be for you! Each pre-flight briefing consists of a number things, including explanations of the flight ahead, the passenger loads, any special requirements such as disabled passengers or VIP's, weather, delays etc. It is also a chance for the purser, senior crew member or manager (titles dependent on specific airline) to check your suitability to fly.

They will check that you are suitable to fly through visually checking that you have your airport ID and passport (without these you are going nowhere!). They will then check that your knowledge is up to date. This will consist of a number of questions being asked, of which you must correctly answer. You are likely to be asked about red notices, SEP and AVMED. Some typical questions that you may be asked are listed below;

 ✈ What is the most recent red notice?

 ✈ If you had to gain emergency access to the flight deck, what code would you enter to open the door?

 ✈ If somebody had a heart attack, what would you do?

 ✈ If you were giving CPR to a baby, how many rescue breaths should you give them?

 ✈ Your colleague has discovered a fire onboard the aircraft, they have called for you, what is your role?

 ✈ How do you open the over wing exit in an emergency?

What would you do to prepare the cabin for a planned ditching?

What medication would you hand out if a passenger had angina?

How would you deal with a passenger that has a chemical product in their eye?

What position would you put somebody in if they have fainted?

There are a huge range of questions that could be asked during the pre-flight briefing and it goes without saying that some managers/ pursers do tend to ask more difficult questions than others. It is important that you keep your knowledge up to date after you have completed your initial training course and do not forget what you have learned. Fortunately, it is not very often that crew will use a lot of the things they learnt during their SEP and AVMED training, however this can mean that you begin to forget things. It is for this reason that you must regularly review your manuals to ensure that you keep your knowledge up to speed!

If you answer questions wrong during your pre-flight briefing it can be problematic. Although most airlines will allow you to forget the answer to one, or maybe even two questions, if you do not demonstrate sufficient knowledge you will be grounded. If you are grounded on this basis you can get in a lot of trouble and will often be asked to undertake a refresher course. However this opportunity will not be given time and time again! Get the questions wrong on several occasions and you will almost certainly be out of the job... so remember, revisit your manuals and make sure you know your stuff!

Cabin Crew Duties

Although the life of a cabin crew member is never dull as you are likely to be in a different part of world each week, serving customers from different cultures and nationalities and working with different crew each shift, there is a surprisingly rigid routine that you will be asked to follow. This is explained below;

Pre-flight checks

Crew will board the aircraft before passengers and check that it is suitable to fly. Whilst pilots will check the operational practicalities, crew will check the security of the aircraft. This includes checking SEP equipment, checking the catering has been loaded and ensuring that the aircraft has been suitably cleaned. Some airlines may ask crew to clean the aircraft themselves, such as budget carriers.

For more information on pre-flight checks see the SEP section in Chapter Two.

Boarding

This is the first time that your passengers will meet you and as such it forms the passenger's first impression of you and the forthcoming flight. Did you know a person decides whether they like somebody they meet within the first 10 seconds? This just shows how crucial those first impressions are!

During boarding each crew member will be allocated a position. They will stand and greet passengers, check their boarding cards if they are located at the main entrance and help passengers to find their seats/ with luggage etc when needed. It is a legal requirement that a crew member covers each set of doors on the aircraft during boarding, and so most airlines will have specific places for each crew member to position themselves depending on their working position.

If working in a premier cabin (each airline will have their own style and names for their cabins, such as 'Upper' or 'First'), you may be required to do other duties during boarding such as handing out newspapers, offering champagne and hanging up passenger's jackets.

Safety demonstration

The safety demo is an integral part of the flying experience as it aims to prepare passengers in the event of an emergency. It takes place whilst the aircraft is taxiing, before take off. Although many passengers may choose not to pay attention, it is a legal requirement that all airlines carry out a safety demo. This can be pre-recorded or undertaken manually by the crew and each crew member will have their own dedicated flight demo position on the aircraft.

For more information on how the flight demo is done, see Chapter Two.

✈ Welcome
After take off the senior crew member will normally do a formal PA to welcome all passengers onboard. This includes general information about the flight ahead and should introduce passengers to the crew onboard.

✈ Meal service
Each flight will normally have a meal service. This may be complimentary if on a scheduled flight, pre paid as is often the case on charter flights or it may be optional (and often costly) as is common on budget airlines. Despite airline food having a reputation for not being very nice, some airlines do offer very good meals, particularly in premier cabins. For instance, First class passengers on British Airway's flights are able to choose their dining options from an al a carte menu that includes foods such as fois gras, lobster or truffles.

The meal service will differ greatly depending on what class you are working in. If working in an economy cabin you may simply offer options of chicken or beef and hand out a tray of food. Alternatively, if working in a premier cabin you may be required to give advice on choice of wine and mix cocktails.

Airline food is difficult to make as your taste buds change onboard an aircraft due to the increase in altitude. It is for this reason that airlines often put a lot of work into the taste of their food, ensuring that it tastes just as good at 30,000ft as it does on the ground.

Airline food is always pre-cooked and reheated onboard the aircraft. There are ovens and sometimes microwaves in the galley areas of the aircraft that crew will use to heat the food. It is important that food is cooked properly as wide spread food poisoning onboard an aircraft, with only a few toilets, could be a disaster! Crew are provided with equipment to test that the food is thoroughly cooked before handing out. Additionally, it is important that food is cooked quickly and efficiently. Onboard a very short flight for instance, crew may part cook the meals on the ground before take off to ensure that there is enough time to complete the service in the air.

✈ Bar service
Each airline will offer a bar service, sometimes drinks are complimentary and other times passengers will be asked to pay for them. Sometimes only non-alcoholic drinks are complimentary, this differs according to the airline.

Depending on the flight, crew may go out with one, or multiple bar services. Passengers are also entitled to ask for drinks by pressing their call bell. Depending on the airline you are working for you will need to learn their service standards- do you need to use a doyly? Do you service women before men or window to aisle? Is the wine bottle allowed to touch the glass?

✈ 'Gashing in'
A term most of you probably haven't heard before that is used daily by crew is the word gash. This essentially means rubbish, and 'gashing in' is the term used when the crew take the gash trolley down the aisle and collect any rubbish.

✈ Duty free service
This is often your opportunity to make some money! Some flights will naturally have more passengers requiring duty free products than others, some days you could make £1 in commission and another you could make £100!

You will normally have a selection of duty free products available for purchase onboard your flight ranging from children's toys and boxes of chocolates, to jewellery, perfume and designer bags. Several crew members will normally be selected to operate the duty free trolley and they will need to carry a float to enable them to hand out change. This is when your maths skills will come in handy as people often want to pay in different currencies which can get quite confusing!

If you are good at selling you can make lots of commission through duty free, which can help to boost your salary. It may be worthwhile familiarising yourself with the onboard products offered by your airline to help you to do this.

✈ Crew rest

Depending on the length of the flight, you may have the opportunity for crew rest. Larger aircraft are likely to have a crew rest area that may have high comfort rest seats or beds for the crew. Crew rest can last from a few minutes to several hours depending on the length of the flight and the needs of the passengers.

✈ Night flights

Night flights, some love them and some hate them! If you are working for a short haul airline this may not apply to you, but if you fly to long haul destinations you will almost certainly be required to work through the night at times! Many airlines will schedule their flights to fly through the night due to time differences, for instance flights returning from America to the UK will often be overnight, given that the UK are ahead in time. On a night flight you will often offer two meal services; dinner and then breakfast shortly before landing.

Some crew love night flights as the passengers are normally tired and they will go to sleep, making your job easier! However, other crew hate them. Although you will normally get some crew rest time, this is likely to only be an hour or two and the rest of the flight you will need to stay awake and alert. Most crew will have a sleep in the afternoon before a night flight, but some find this easier than others. They will then sleep in the day time after they have landed. This can disrupt your sleep pattern and make it difficult to get some 'shut eye' at reasonable hours.

✈ Administration/ paperwork

Although you may choose to work as cabin crew to avoid the likes of admin, you can never really get away from it! There are various documents that crew must complete during the flight. Below are some examples;

🛬 Incident report form
This is completed if there is an onboard incident, for instance a drunk passenger or an injury.

🛬 Flight report
This is paperwork that outlines anything relevant that has happened on the flight.

🛬 Duty free/ bar paperwork
Many airlines will require crew to count the products left at the end of a flight and to seal any carts using a plastic seal, the seal number will then be recorded. This helps to minimise theft once the products are taken off the aircraft.

🛬 Disembarkation
At the end of the flight you will say goodbye to your passengers. It is at this moment that you will often get 'mouth ache' from smiling for such a long period of time! It can take a while to get all passengers off the aircraft and some passengers may need assistance. If there are wheelchair passengers or anybody requiring ground assistance you will be required to wait with them until the relevant person comes to take over from you.

Working Positions

On each flight crew will be given a working position. This is usually ranked by seniority and will begin with the most senior crew member as number one. The size of the aircraft will depend on how many operating crew are onboard. Here are a couple of examples of how seniority may work;

🛬 Boeing 747
The jumbo jet will normally have in the range of 14-18 crew members onboard, depending on passenger loads and seating configurations (The CAA states that there should be at least one crew member for each set of doors and a minimum of 1 crew member for every 50 passengers onboard).

On a 747 the airline will have a manager as number one, titles vary depending on the airline examples include CSM (Cabin Service Manager) if working for British Airways Mixed Fleet or FSM (Flight Service Manager) if working for Virgin Atlantic. There will normally then be some senior crew members that are known as FTC (Future Talent Crew) at BA Mixed Fleet or Pursers at many other airlines. There will generally be a senior crew member (or acting senior member if appropriate) in each cabin who will manage the crew and workloads in that area. Finally, the remaining crew will be numbered according to their preferred position or as directed by the onboard manager.

As a 747 is a large aircraft, different crew members will have different responsibilities. For instance, the number 10 might be in charge of handing out children's entertainment packs and a number four might be in charge of looking after UNMINS (unaccompanied minors). This helps to ensure that every job is undertaken efficiently and to manage workloads. When training, you will learn about the different working positions and their responsibilities and you will need to learn these before your first flight.

✈ Airbus A319

This is one of the smaller aircraft that crew are likely to operate and as such requires far less crew. It is typical that there may only be three crew members operating this aircraft. The number one will be the manager or purser (title dependent on the airline) and the number two and three will generally be ranked according to their experience and duration that they have worked for the airline. Again, each crew member will have their own individual responsibilities, for example the number two may do the PA's and the number three may operate the duty free.

Classes

If working for a scheduled airline, you are likely to have the option of working in different classes (also sometimes referred to as cabins). Each airline differs in terms of configurations and names. For instance, Virgin Atlantic flights generally offer three classes of travel; Economy, Premium Economy and Upper. Alternatively, British Airways generally offers four classes on their long haul flights; World Traveller, World Traveller Plus, Club and First.

Each airline will have their own method of determining what class their crew work in. Some may do it in order of seniority and length of service, for instance when working for Virgin Atlantic you are likely to spend your first couple of years working in the economy cabin and then work your way up. On the other hand, some airlines like to offer their crew variety and give them the option of working in different cabins on every flight if they choose to, this is something that British Airways Mixed Fleet promotes.

Whilst undertaking your initial cabin crew training you will learn the different service routines in each cabin (if applicable). The services can be quite different so it is important that you learn these- after all, it wouldn't be very good customer service if you started offering an economy service in first class would it!

Uniforms

One of the first things you generally notice when you see cabin crew is their uniform. Cabin crew are the face of the airline and as such, airlines take a lot of pride in their appearance. Uniforms are specially designed to meet the needs of crew and some airlines go to great lengths to ensure that their crew 'look the part'. For example, the British Airways uniforms are designed by fashion celebrity Julian MacDonald and Virgin Atlantic has recently hired Vivienne Westwood to design their new uniform!

You can instantly recognise what airline somebody works for by their uniform. Are they dressed in red with red high heels? Do they have a bright orange scarf and shirt? Or do they sport a red hat with draping veil? Cabin crew are marketing the airline just by wearing the uniform!

Airlines generally have very strict uniform standards, and although these differ slightly between airlines, they are all usually very strict as you are 'the face of the airline'. If you boarded a flight and were welcomed with a crew member with an unironed shirt, ladder in her tights and scruffy hair, what would be your impression of the airline? A bit sloppy perhaps? Uniform says everything, so airlines want their crew to look professional and smart at all times!

Below are some typical guidelines for uniform standards that you may come across whilst working as cabin crew, although of course standards depend on the individual airline's uniform;

✈ Hair

Your hair must always be neat and tidy. The airline may have specific requirements such as that it must be tied up in a bun using a donut (you can buy these in shops such as Boots or Superdrug). If coloured, the hair must look natural and roots much be maintained. Airlines will often have specific requirements about the colour of hair ties or grips used and there must not be any loose strands of hair or long fringes. Men's hair must be short and neat, facial hair must be trimmed/ cleanly shaven.

✈ Make up

Women are generally encouraged to wear make up and some airlines make this an essential requirement. Make up must use natural colours and will often need to include lipstick. Some airlines will give cabin crew training on how to do their make up during their initial training course and they may even have specially designed make up items that they hand out to cabin crew as part of the uniform (Virgin Atlantic have their own lipstick!). Cabin crew are expected to reapply make up when applicable throughout the flight, especially after they have been for a sleep during their crew rest! When buying make up you may want to purchase a long wearing foundation so that it lasts the duration of the flight; many crew choose Estee Lauder Double Wear or similar. Your skin will become very dry whilst flying so you may also want to purchase a good moisturiser.

Perfume
Wear perfume.... Just not too much!

Jewellery
Each airline will have their own specific requirements, but as a general rule of thumb, a small ring on each hand, a watch and one pair of earings is standard. Airlines normally require watches to be smart and not too large.

Nails
As crew, your nails should always be neat and tidy. Your airline will normally ask you to have natural coloured nails or to paint them in a colour that is complimentary of the uniform. Many crew will have their nails done professionally. If you do choose to paint your own nails, make sure that you take the nail polish to work with you, because chipped nail polish is a big no go!

As crew you will be working with your hands a lot, so although having nice long nails looks great, you do need to ensure that they are practical too.

Tights
Most airlines will require you to wear tights as part of the uniform and will specify what denier you should wear. As tights are easily laddered, it is important that you always pack a spare pair of tights in your bag. Many cabin crew will also pack clear nail polish and this can be used on any small holes to prevent a ladder forming.

Tattoos
Tattoos are generally a big no go for cabin crew and it is usually a prerequisite of being offered the job that any body art is declared in the initial application form (this was discussed in Chapter One). Having said that, many crew do have tattoos that they choose to hide using tattoo cover up makeup or items of clothing. Generally, as long as the tattoo is

not visable it shouldn't be a problem, but if you are aspiring cabin crew and you have a tattoo up your arm, along your foot, on your neck, ankle, wrist or anywhere else it can be seen then you may want to start booking some tattoo removal sessions! Also, be careful of tattoos on your body that may be seen through a white shirt!

✈ Shoes
Cabin crew will normally have more than one pair of shoes; heels for walking through the airport and boarding and flats (well almost, a small heel is usually fine) for onboard the aircraft. This is because if there was an emergency evacuation high heels may rip the slides. Also, high heels would hurt your feet when walking around all flight- you'd be surprised how many miles crew clock up in a day walking up and down the aisles!

Your airline may provide you with shoes or they may give specific requirements for shoes that you should purchase yourself. These shoes can sometimes be a little tricky to find in the shops, a good place to look is www.cabinshoes.com.

✈ Airline uniform
The specific uniform details will be explained to you by your airline during your training. You will normally be given uniform free of charge, although if you may need to pay for any additional items you require. Your trainers will teach you things such as how to tie your cravat or scarf if you have one or how to wear your hat. Your airline will expect you to meet the uniform standards and wear your uniform correctly at all times.

You are representing the airline for the duration of the time that you are wearing your uniform. It is for this reason that many airlines will ask you to conform to full uniform standards, even if you are no longer on duty. Thinking about taking your scarf off and untucking your shirt before popping to the supermarket on your way home? Think again! Although you may no longer be on duty, if you are seen you can face disciplinary action for not adhering to uniform standards. This stands for photographs you put online or on social media too.

Changing Jobs

Had enough of flying? No problem! One of the biggest benefits to working for an airline are the career opportunities that are provided. From working in reservations, to customer services, to flight service management, cabin crew training or marketing, opportunities within airlines are abundant. Many airlines offer their staff the opportunity to take secondments, whereby they are able to undertake a different job within the company for a period of time. They also offer many internal opportunities for movement to different roles within the airline.

Promotion Prospects

Most airlines will offer very good promotion prospects. Many crew who choose to are able to progress to senior positions within the airline after a period of time. Promotion prospects vary according to airlines, some may require crew to work for them for a longer period of time than others before they are able to be promoted, whereas others offer very fast progression. An example of fast progression is the new BA Mixed Fleet, where there are a number of people that are promoted to FTC or CSM within only a few months of commencing work for the airline.

In Flight Assessments

Whilst working for an airline the managers will need to monitor your performance which will often be done through IFAs (in flight assessments). This is when a member of senior cabin crew will observe your performance throughout the flight and give you developmental feedback, a bit like an formal observation.

You will have to have regular IFAs and the exact length of time between assessments will depend on the airline you work for. Some airlines will link your IFA feedback to a bonus or pay increment, giving you that extra incentive to deliver your best service at all times. Some airline managers will notify you that they are planning on observing you, whilst others may not.

Pregnancy and Babies

For many women, when they decide to settle down and have a family, they also decide that it is time to stop flying. Although this may be the preferred option for some people, flying can still work well for others.

Airlines are generally very supportive of their crew members that choose to have babies and the moment the crew member notifies the airline that they are pregnant they will be allocated ground duties. This is because the risk of miscarrying can increase with regular flying, particularly during the early stages of pregnancy. Whilst pregnant, crew may be asked to work in a variety of positions including in the offices, on customer services or in the crew report center.

Crew will be given maternity leave and then asked to return to work after a period of time (usually 6-12 months). Some or all of the maternity leave will be paid. If you choose, there is normally the option to request to reduce your hours to part time on your return to work. Part time rosters differ depending on the airline, some work one month on one month off, some work ten days per month and others may only work particular shifts. If you are interested in reducing your hours you will need to discuss this with your line manager.

Many crew however continue to work as they did before having their baby, with the help and support of their family. Many people enjoy working as crew and make their rosters work for their family life through bidding for particular flights and arranging child care whilst they are away.

Celebrities

What's your claim to fame? Did you serve Victoria Beckham a fruit salad or make Tom Jones' bed? Or maybe Prince Harry complimented you on your scrambled eggs? Working as cabin crew can introduce you to many people that you would not normally meet!

HOWEVER... airlines are very particular about what you can and cannot say about the celebrities you meet onboard. They are also particular about the way you behave. You may want to run up to Ed Sheeran screaming and asking for his autograph, but this type of behavior is an absolute NO! You must remain professional and polite at all times.

Many celebrities choose to fly with particular airlines because of their level of professionalism, and as such the airline will expect you to uphold that reputation. That means not taking any sneaky photographs of them when they are not looking, not taking home the passenger manifest to frame and not publically announcing your experiences on the likes of Facebook or Twitter! If you do not follow the rules you can face disciplinary action or even dismissal.

Time Down Route

The time down route is one of the biggest reasons that people choose to become cabin crew. Do you want to see the world? Working as cabin crew is definitely one way to do it! However, is not as 'all signing, all dancing' as you might think.

Depending on the airline that you work for and the destination you are flying to, you may have a little or a lot of time down route. For instance, you might land into Paris at 10pm and leave again at 10am, and although you may fit in a quick round of drinks at the hotel bar before bed, you haven't really got much opportunity to sightsee. On the other hand, you might fly to Los Angeles and have two full days to entertain yourself. You can go out partying in Hollywood, pay a trip to Disney or relax on Venice Beach.

However, although having days down route may sound great, you also need to manage your time and money to ensure that you can go out and enjoy yourself. Due to the low salaries offered by some airlines, many crew will opt to pack food items such as porridge pots or cereal bars to help their money go further. They also may choose not to go out and to save money instead.

Although being cabin crew can be really, really fun, it can also be a very, very lonely job. Did you know that cabin crew is the world's number one occupation for committing suicide? What a scary fact! When working as crew you may not always want to go out, you may not always have the money or you may just be feeling homesick. When working as cabin crew you can get very lonely as you are likely to be flying with different people every shift, making it quite difficult to make friends! People that work as cabin crew are generally independent people, people that are outgoing and that make friends easily. If you are an isolated or shy person you may feel very lonely.

If you want to make the most of your time down route you might also need to plan your sleep. Many destinations that you are likely to fly to will have significant time differences, meaning that you may need to stay awake when your body is telling you to sleep in order to get out and explore the destination you are in. You will also need to make sure that you get some down time before a night flight, and so you may need to make some time whilst down route for a quick cat nap.

Many crew love to drink, and the hotel bar is often one of the first places that will be visited upon arriving in a new destination. Many airlines will also give crew the opportunity to buy 'crew purchase', this is when cabin crew buy alcohol from the aircraft at a heavily discounted rate.

As cabin crew you will often be given the opportunity to visit places of the world that you would never normally choose, making it a very exciting job! To read more about the different destinations visited and activities that can be undertaken whilst as crew visit the website www.lifeasabutterfly.com.

The Highs and Lows of Being Cabin Crew

Overall, working as cabin crew can be a fantastic job, however as with anything there are always positives and negatives. Below is a summary of the highs and lows of working as cabin crew discussed throughout this book;

Highs

    ✈ Not a 9-5 job

    ✈ Every day is different

    ✈ Meet new people every day

    ✈ Travel the world!!!

    ✈ Opportunity to boost earnings through commission

    ✈ Customer facing role

    ✈ Wide range of staff benefits including discounted/ free flights

    ✈ Free uniforms
    ✈ Opportunity to meet people you wouldn't usually, such as celebrities

    ✈ Working for a world renowned company

    ✈ Comprehensive cabin crew training

Lows

    ✈ Can be difficult to maintain social life

    ✈ Disturbed sleep patterns

✈ Difficult to plan in advance

✈ Last minute roster changes

✈ Difficult to make friends

✈ Low salaries

✈ Can be a lonely job

✈ Difficult training course to complete

Conclusion

Working as cabin crew really is a job like no other, and although there may be some negative aspects to the job, for many, the positives far outweigh them! Do you want to look glamorous at work? Do you enjoy providing a high level of customer service? Do you like meeting new people? Do you like variety? Do you love travel? Then cabin crew may well be the perfect job for you!

From the initial application process, to the training course and providing an excellent service when on line, working as cabin crew is very much the 'unknown' for a number of aspiring crew members. This book outlines all of the essential information that any prospective crew member will need to know. For further information on life as cabin crew and 'real life tales' visit the website www.lifeasabutterfly.com.

CPSIA information can be obtained
at www.ICGtesting.com
Printed in the USA
LVHW08s2105011018
592013LV00013B/1392/P